S0-BCQ-810

Shaped to Its Purpose

Delta Sigma Theta — The first fifty years

by Mary Elizabeth Vroman

Published in New York by Random House,Inc., and simultaneously in Toronto, Canada, by Random House of Canada Limited.
Library of Congress Catalog Card Number: 64-8777
Manufactured in the United States of America by H. Wolff, N.Y.

Acknowledgments

The history of a relatively small society, as is any fraternal organization, differs in many respects from that of a larger society such as a race, a region, or a nation. The author of a history of the United States, for example, would find innumerable sources of reference for his compilation. In our case, almost all the information about Delta Sigma Theta Sorority has been drawn from records in the archives at Delta's headquarters in Washington, D. C. Therefore, this history is presented without footnotes or bibliography.

But certain acknowledgements and credits are necessary. The author wishes to express her thanks to the living Founders, who so willingly contributed their recollections of the early days of the sorority; Edna Johnson Morris, First Grand Historian, whose *History and Development of Delta Sigma Theta Sorority,* published in August, 1944, supplied much of the "lost" information about Delta's first decade; the painstaking recording secretaries, whose detailed accounts of the National Conventions have facilitated this record; all contributors to the *Delta Journal* and other Delta publications whose reports and articles have been incorporated into this history; Dr. John Hope Franklin, Professor of History at the University of Chicago, and noted historian, whose help has been invaluable in exploring the social implications and influences that have contributed to the composition and outlook of Delta Sigma Theta; Mary Elizabeth Carnegie, Associate Editor of *Nursing Outlook*, the official organization of The National League for Nurses, and recent Chairman of the sorority's Publications and Public Relations Committee, so often and gratefully consulted; and not least, the Staff at Delta's Headquarters, without whose patient assistance the research for this book could not have been done at all.

M. E. V.
New York City
November 1964

Acknowledgments

Second Printing

In our charge to keep each generation of Deltas knowledgeable of our past and because of the numerous queries received as we traveled the most recent regional conference cycle, the National Heritage and Archives Committee initiated the efforts to reprint the first fifty years of our history. This book has been out of print since 1972 and many have expressed the desire to own a copy for personal libraries.

Here it is!

I would like to offer thanks to the 1992-93 National Executive Board for endorsing the initiative, to Soror Roseline McKinney, Executive Director, and headquarters staff for their patience and assistance; to the "ever ready to serve" Heritage and Archives Committee, namely, Sorors Fabette T. D. Smith (Co-Chair), Elsie Atwell, Yvonne Catchings, Marlese Durr, Allie Miller Holley, Sonja McGill, Betsy Pearson, Emily Rickman, Lela Roberts, Sharon Snow, Charlie Mae Smith, Lavoise Smith, Valencia Faye Tate, Carol Ware, Grace White-Ware, Garlenda McNair (Headquarters Staff Liaison) and to Soror Avril L'Mour Weathers for her volunteer efforts.

We hope that this book will serve as an inspiration to continue our commitment to a preservation of our legacy.

Ella Goode Johnson, Chair
National Heritage and Archives Committee (1992-94)

Contents

Foreword ix

1 SHAPED TO ITS PURPOSE 3
Delta Sigma Theta: Through the looking-glass

2 THE SEED IS PLANTED 11
The founding of Delta Sigma Theta

3 THE SAPLING GROWS 19
Organizing and expanding

4 FLINGS WIDE ITS BRANCHES 33
Becoming an instrument of public service

5 THE ROOTS ARE SECURE 61
Delta: A mature organization

6 HEARD IS ITS SINGING 81
Fun, fellowship, and fund-raising

7 IN TUNE WITH ITS BROTHERS 95
Co-operating with other organizations

8 BY YIELDING ITS FRUITS 107
Delta's five public service projects

9 IN MULTIPLE HARVEST 139
Delta dividends

10 THE TREE CAN ENDURE 153
Implications for the future

APPENDICES 184
A. Founders 184
B. Honorary members 185
C. Grand presidents and terms of office 186
D. Conventions: Dates, locales and major emphases 187
E. Chapters and dates of establishment 191

INDEX 207

Foreword

Delta Sigma Theta Sorority has been marked with so many facts and events related to its development since its inception, that a history of its first half-century could well be a volume impressive in wealth of detail and in size; and because of its impressiveness, it might well remain on the shelves of its owners, unread except for such times as it might be needed as a source of reference.

This history, therefore, is not designed to be a total repository of Delta information, much of which is recorded elsewhere. While it does seek to supply all facts of major importance, its main object is to present to the non-member and to all members, present and future, a clear and objective record of what the organization was and is, and of what it has attempted to accomplish in its first fifty years in existence.

Delta Sigma Theta Sorority, by its own expressed ideals, accepts an active responsibility for the betterment of the society in which it exists. Thus it is hoped that this history may serve as an aid in determining how the sorority has measured up to the challenge of changing patterns through the years.

This book is dedicated to every member of Delta Sigma Theta — but chiefly to the neophytes, the newest Deltas of each year. It is dedicated in the hope that in tracing from its pages what Delta was and is and hopes to become, each Delta may be inspired to add her individual torch to the larger flame of loving service — which is the Spirit of Delta.

Foreword
Second Printing

Delta Sigma Theta Sorority, Inc., is a public service sorority founded on Christian principles by twenty-two collegiate women at Howard University in 1913. These Founders were influenced by social, political and economic contingencies which molded their lives and the early life of the Sorority. Thus, Delta Sigma Theta was "Shaped to Its Purpose."

Delta was shaped by twenty-two American women of African descent determined to serve their communities in the face of overt subjugation, massive poverty, and expansive migration. Delta was shaped by nineteenth century Victorian images of womanhood, the strength of a Black Women's Club Movement, and a redefined notion of Black Womanhood. Delta was shaped by popularized segregationist policies of the state, and sanctioned violence in our communities. Delta was shaped by the rise of an industrialist economy and the exclusion of Black workers from both industrial and union life. Delta Sigma Theta Sorority, Inc., was indeed "Shaped to Its Purpose."

The significance of our first fifty years is more than that of an historical recording. It is an investigation into the provision of service through some of the most difficult historical passages that this country has experienced. From the dominance of agriculture to the explosion of industry, from the great war over Africa to the great war over Europe, from the Great Depression to the post-world war economic boom, and from the evolution of Plessy to the resolution of Brown, this nation's trends shifted more completely in those fifty years than in any fifty year period before or since — and Delta Sigma Theta was in service every step of the way.

Now that we have become a force that shapes society as well as being shaped by it, members have been inquiring about the availability of this history and a second printing was set in motion to accommodate this popular request. The value of this edition rests with the fact that it is the Sorority's first historical record, and not necessarily with the accuracy of this record. What you are about to experience is the original and unaltered text of "Shaped to Its Purpose: Delta Sigma Theta, The First Fifty Years."

Bertha M. Roddey, Ph.D.
20th National President
May 1994

Shaped to its purpose
The seed is planted.
The sapling grows—
Flings wide its branches
The roots are secure.

Heard is its singing
In tune with its brothers.
By yielding its fruits
In multiple harvest
The tree can endure.

"We are shaped by our purpose, that of forming a closer union among college women for the fostering of high ideals in moral, social and intellectual life, and the assisting of our members. . . ."

Patricia Roberts Harris
Executive Director's Report
24th National Convention, 1956

1 *Shaped to its purpose*

Delta Sigma Theta: through the looking-glass

DELTA: WHAT AND WHY

Delta Sigma Theta is a national Greek-letter society with 272 chapters located in 36 states including Alaska, in the District of Columbia, the Republic of Haiti, and Liberia, West Africa. The 32,000 members, of whom 8,000 are active and financial, who currently comprise Delta Sigma Theta Sorority have come mainly from Negro colleges. It must be remembered then, in tracing the first fifty years in the history of this organization, that although Delta Sigma Theta bears a status similar to that of any other American college sorority, it has been continuously shaped in form and purpose to meet the needs of Negro college women.

For long decades after the Civil War the Negro woman endured what was probably the lowest position in America's social structure. In the South, where white womanhood was placed on a pedestal, the Negro woman was accorded neither honor for her womanhood nor respect for her person. With no legal protection, she was ever the prey of the salacious male, white or black. Too often she was given choice neither of husband nor of the father of her children; and it was to be several decades after Emancipation before her position was greatly changed. It is therefore an obvious tribute to her basic nobility that by dint of dogged, almost militant determination, she has managed to achieve and maintain a successively higher status.

The post-bellum era predictably was a difficult one for the American Negro. The Emancipation Proclamation had brought him, not only his long-desired freedom, but a perhaps somewhat frightening personal responsibility. Suddenly he had to acquire knowledges and skills hitherto forbidden him. He was used to hard labor; but the same labor was now rewarded by pitifully small wages that must somehow be managed in order to provide the food, shelter, and clothing—however poor in quality—previously provided by the master.

The ex-slave grasped, however dimly, the struggle toward true citizenship that lay before him; and he grasped also that the struggle was now almost totally his. If his American citizenship was to be more than nominal, he must adapt his morals and mores to the new culture, and enable himself to stand equal in achievement with other Americans. He saw education as the chief means toward this end. The man of the family who worked all day in the fields or at his trade had little time for more than making a living. Although the wife worked too, more often than not, it was her additional responsibility to maintain the family unit, to introduce to her household the ways she had learned in the house of her white mistress, and to encourage and inspire her children to desire and seek more and more of the white man's skills and learnings. In short, the woman was the hub of the family. It is little wonder that there resulted among Negroes what amounted to a matriarchal society that was to remain such for a considerable time.

An additional factor in making this true was that for some time Negro women were to outstrip their men in educational achievement. Schooling for boys was limited, for they were obliged to reach an early manhood in order to help their fathers support the family. Moreover, it was considered more important to use the family savings to equip the girls to take care of themselves: The boys would manage, if only by reason of their male strength. Thus, at the turn of the century, women were in the large majority in Negro colleges, and, within the race, Negro womanhood had earned a status worthy of respect and admiration.

Simultaneously on the larger American scene women were coming into their own and were demanding suffrage, breaking into professions which had been considered the exclusive calling of men, and generally seeking equal freedom for self-development and self-expression.

Delta Sigma Theta, founded in 1913 by twenty-two Howard University undergraduates, was an outgrowth of the times. In common with other American sororities, Delta provided a means for a member to maintain a closer affiliation with her peers in interests and achievements, and lent to the member the distinction of belonging to a somewhat exclusive group. In general, sororities were seen as symbols of the status sought by women. But the Negro soror had then, and still has, needs more pressing than mere status-seeking. The well-educated Negro woman, able to find few other outlets for her potential for leadership and service through affiliation with the kinds of groups open to whites, soon saw the sorority as a means of serving first the immediate community, and ultimately the larger communities of race, region, and nation.

In the year of her founding, Delta Sigma Theta listed as her "particular purpose and object: to establish and maintain a high standard of morality and scholarship among women"; and during the following decade greatest stress was laid on scholastic achievement and mutual enjoyment of cultural and social activities. But as her numbers grew, Delta was to move from mere self-concern to the realization of the possibilities for service in ever-widening areas, so that she now lists herself as a Public Service Organization rather than a "social" sorority.

It is significant that Delta's greater perspectives are still considered consonant with the original goals set by the founders, and that the present Constitution more specifically explains Delta goals, but in no way contradicts them. Then, as now, active contribution on behalf of one's fellow men was considered a major aspect of morality.

RELATIONSHIPS: INTERNAL AND EXTERNAL

The minority usually reflects the whole, and the fraternal organization is sometimes as denounced on Negro campuses as on white, and for much the same reasons. On occasion, on certain campuses, it has been felt that sorority activities interfere with maximum scholastic achievement. In view of an educational program which avowedly seeks to develop the "whole" man and woman, it is difficult to gauge the merit of such an argument. But Delta makes a consistent effort to ensure that her program is a spur rather than a handicap to scholastic achievement. Moreover, the sorority has taken firm steps to outlaw all initiation practices meriting censure.

Much of the argument against sororities in general is that they promote an undemocratic caste system on and off the campus, and there is some indication that, for this reason, the fraternal organization is on the wane on the American scene. Delta leadership has given thoughtful consideration to the future of the organization. The possibility has been faced that the society may not survive another half-century as a sorority. In an age of greater technical needs and demands, she may develop into an organization with so wide a scope that she no longer can be considered a sorority. Already certain departures have been made, and Delta's current program exceeds what are usually considered the bounds of sorority activity. In her growing concern for the public welfare, Delta Sigma Theta now omits the word "sorority" in all advertising, and employs the slogan, Delta Sigma Theta—Dedicated to Public Service.

Consideration has also been given to the role Delta plays as a predominantly Negro group. Because of the narrow scope of social and civic outlets, Negro women continue to identify actively with the sorority after graduation, in contrast to most white college women, whose postgraduate affiliation with their sororities is usually nominal. Delta thus faced the prospect of becoming alumae dominated; and alert to the danger she established, in 1959, a special committee known as the Yancey Commission on Undergraduate Development, which was to investigate undergraduate status in relation to the whole sorority, and to take steps to ensure that the role of the Delta undergraduate is not subordinated to that of the alumna. This was done, not in an effort to minimize the activity of the alumna, on whom rests the major responsibility for carrying out Delta's program, but with the realization that undergraduates are the basis of the organization, and are vital to its effectiveness and continuance. For it is supposed that whatever form or shape Delta may assume in the coming years, her membership will continue to consist largely of college-bred women. Because the purpose of Delta Sigma Theta is service, her membership is chosen with an eye to capacity for leadership. Therefore it always has been required that the initiate maintain a high scholastic record. Only to this extent and to that of demanding moral fitness does Delta consider herself exclusive.

Progress in desegregation, evident in this decade throughout the nation, presents new challenges to Delta. Chapters have been established on interracial campuses where now she must compete with larger and more renowned sororities for new members. Early in Delta's history, one of her most famous members foresaw the changes to come in race relations. Mary Church Terrell, who fought valiantly for equal human rights, urged Delta to become inclusive in attitude and welcome any woman having the necessary qualifications into the ranks, regardless of race or color. Much credit can be given her for the sorority's increased capacity for self-appraisal.

On interracial campuses, Delta is confronted by additional odds in competing with white sororities for membership, because she is unable to afford the maintenance of Delta Houses on campuses where sorority members are required to live in their respective sorority houses. Furthermore, the official position of Delta's National Board is that major investments in chapter housing are lowest in budget priority, because of the many more urgent problems to be tackled in Negro communities. Hence Delta finds it understandable when a Negro undergraduate chooses membership in a white sorority. Individual freedom of choice, based on personal preference, is what the Negro seeks. Should the sorority suffer a loss to white sororities in prospective membership, she is heartened by the possibility of new racial elements being introduced into her own group. Already a small number of white women and women of other races have membership in Delta Sigma Theta.

Delta's widened horizons have brought her the additional satisfaction of harmonious working relationships with other predominantly Negro fraternal organizations. Initially, rivalries among Negro sororities were so intense that frequently each existed in proud isolation. Now, happily, there exists among them a growing willingness to join forces and work together for specific common goals. Progress in this area will be dealt with more fully in Chapter 7.

FUNCTIONS AND FACTORS

In the first half-century of her existence Delta has seen great changes in the patterns of living in the United States and throughout the world. That she has survived and thrived through these changes has been due largely to her capacity, engendered by wise leadership, for adapting her program to meet the needs of the times. And although she reviews her history with some pride in past achievements, her chief aim is to appraise her actions in the past and her functions in the present so that she may be guided into a well-planned and contributing future, and thus continue to justify her existence.

Delta functions in much the same manner as does the democracy from which she derives. As the individual contributes to the existence and welfare of the whole, so does the whole contribute to the welfare of the individual. As a body, Delta seeks to develop in the individual soror those qualities that will contribute to greater self-realization—through the developed individual to make effective contribution to the outside world.

On chapter level, the smallest group unit in the organization, greatest stress is laid on serving the distinct needs of the Negro community—the immediate outside level of Delta concern. On regional level, the area of concern widens to include the combined programs of all chapters contained within the region. And on national level, the sorority views itself in relationship to the total American scene, using its unit influence wherever advisable to promote higher standards in human treatment and better race relations.

Knowing that she is the sum of her composite parts and knowing that she must keep step with national and world progress, within the past decade Delta has launched an internal program unofficially known as "Opening Windows on the World." Educational in part, this program seeks to influence the thinking of the Delta member, and thus that of the whole body, toward an allegiance not limited to race and region, but widened to include the concept of national and world citizenship. That chapters recently have been formed in Haiti, Alaska, and Liberia is some proof of the effectiveness of this program.

2 *The seed is planted*

The founding of Delta Sigma Theta

FOUNDING: HOW AND WHY

In 1912, Alpha Kappa Alpha was the only Negro sorority in the United States. Located at Howard University in Washington, D.C., it had been founded in 1906, and by 1913, there existed two distinct elements in the sorority: the group of college-age graduates, and a group of older students who had finished a two-year course that apparently qualified them to teach grade school in the mornings and to continue their college course at Howard in the afternoons. It followed naturally that members of the latter group were less involved than the former in campus issues. They were also, because of their divided interests, less fired by the enthusiasms of their younger sorors.

This was the era when women throughout the Western world were rebelling against the subordinate status so long accorded them by society and were urgently demanding equal rights under the law. In this country the voice of the feminist movement was, logically, heard most insistently in Washington, D.C., where, amid much controversy, the laws ensuring such equality were being introduced.

The college campus, where intellectual grappling with social and civic issues is encouraged, is often a breeding ground for action in such matters. Howard University, located in the nation's capital, reflected in its students the spirit of the times. Accordingly, the younger members of Alpha Kappa Alpha decided that their affiliation should be devoted to larger matters than those with which they previously had been concerned. It was felt that the times demanded of women everywhere evidence of their emancipated thinking and acting. As women who in the new era would share the responsibility for contributive citizenship, they must now set for themselves new goals which would lift the sorority to higher and wider levels of endeavor than mere fraternal comradship.

With the serious enthusiasm of youth, these college girls set about revamping the total structure of their organization. The more reserved teacher-group, under the leadership of Nellie Quander, took decided exception to the radical changes proposed by their juniors, and immediately took steps to preserve Alpha Kappa Alpha with its original name, aims, and goals. Undismayed, the younger students voted unanimously to adopt as a new title Delta Sigma Theta Sorority, and to incorporate under that name. The reorganization meeting was held January 13,1913, and this date thenceforth was to be celebrated by Delta Sigma Theta as Founders' Day.

Rather naturally, the younger students were considered by the loyal nucleus group as having seceded, and dishonorably at that; while those who now called themselves Delta Sigma Theta felt they had merely reorganized.

For long years thereafter, this was a sore point at issue between the two groups, and much strong rivalry existed between them. It would seem now a happy circumstance, for it is possible that the original group, for lack of competition, might have found little incentive to develop and grow. As it was, the healthy competition encouraged in both groups a continuous widening of horizons, and enabled both to increase in strength and vigor.

The change of name which had so distressed their elders was no mere whim on the part of the young Deltas. The original name had been chosen merely as a Greek symbol. Even so the new group reasoned that Alpha Kappa Alpha, although Greek letters, did not create an instantaneous Greek image to the eye of the uninitiated when written AKA. Delta Sigma Theta, when written ΔΣΘ, was unmistakably Greek, and therefore conveyed the idea that it represented a Greek-letter fraternal organization. Moreover, the new name was chosen carefully to represent the first letters of a secret motto in Greek, reflecting the highest aims of the new sorority.

Much credit must be given to the "young bunch of upstarts," as they were called by the loyal AKA's, for the thoughtful manner in which they proceeded to build the foundation of their new organization. As soon as possible a charter was to be obtained from the parent institution, and legal power sought to form other chapters on other campuses. In view of the plan for extending its ranks beyond Howard University, the Delta Sigma Theta founding body named itself Alpha Chapter of Delta Sigma Theta Sorority. Myra Davis (Hemmings), who had been president of the body before reorganization and who had excellent leadership ability, was elected president of the new sorority. Her term of office expired in May of 1913, when she was graduated; she was succeeded by Madree Penn (White).

INCORPORATION AND OUTGROWTHS

Delta Sigma Theta Sorority was incorporated on February 18, 1913; however, this charter pertained only to Alpha Chapter at Howard University. As chapters were formed on other campuses, they sought individual charters. By 1930, it was evident that it was best to seek incorporation for the entire body, and Grand Chapter was incorporated under the National President, Dr. Anna R. Johnson (Julian).

These early days in the history of Delta Sigma Theta were exciting ones for the young founders. Although duly incorporated, the sorority still had much to do to gain the desired recognition on the Howard campus. Toward this end, Delta asked some outstanding women to come to her assistance, for the newborn sorority recognized the need to assert herself as a significant group on the campus, and hence openly sought sponsors wth prestige. The Founders enlisted the aid of Mrs. Gabrielle Pelham, Mrs. Mary Church Terrell, and Mrs. Nannie H. Burroughs.

Mrs. Gabrielle Pelham had served as the Director of Music at Howard University since 1904, and before that, she had been affiliated with the Conservatory of Music at Adrian, Michigan. She was invited to be the first Honorary Member of Delta Sigma Theta.

Mrs. Mary Church Terrell, the wife of Judge Robert H. Terrell, was a name for Negroes to conjure with. This brilliant and well-educated woman, who had studied in France, Germany, Switzerland, and Italy, was an indefatigable worker for civil rights. Many "firsts" can be claimed by this teacher-lecturer-writer: she was the first woman of her race to serve on the Washington, D.C., Board of Education; she was the first Negro woman chosen to represent the United States Congress of Women, delivering in their name an address in three languages; she was the first president of the National Association of Colored Women. And it was she, acting as chairman of the Co-ordinating Committee for the Enforcement of the District of Columbia Anti-Discrimination Laws, who won a favorable decision from the United States Supreme Court, in upholding the "lost" laws of 1872 and 1873 which banned segregation in Washington restaurants. Inviting Mary Church Terrell to become an honorary member was a stroke of genius on the part of the Delta Founders. She contributed to the new organization not only the prestige of her sponsorship and an integral part of Delta concept—the Delta Oath—but also, by her wise and dynamic guidance, enlarged the thinking and directed the youthful energies of the young Deltas into contributive, constructive channels.

Mrs. Nannie H. Burroughs, another distinguished educator and lecturer, was noted as the founder of the National Training School for Women and Girls in Washington, D.C. She worked for some fifty years with the Baptist World Alliance, and once served as Associate Editor of the *Christian Banner of Philadelphia.* A forceful platform speaker, Mrs. Burroughs was a true pioneer in working to advance the cause of equal rights for women, and her sponsorship as an honorary member was an added spur to the young Founders to work towards this end.

With the addition of these and other prominent women to its honorary ranks, Delta's status was now assured. There was no longer any doubt that the new sorority would flourish.

THE FOUNDERS: RECORDS AND RECOLLECTIONS

Although the twenty-two young women in Alpha Chapter knew the importance of influential supporters in establishing the status of Delta Sigma Theta, they realized that the sorority's future was in their own hands. Honorary members and well-wishers would give support only as long as the organization merited it. With joint determination, the founders began proving their adequacy to this task. Their stated purpose in the Certificate of Incorporation was, "to establish and maintain a high standard of morality and scholarship among women generally, and especially among the women of the School of Liberal Arts at Howard University. . . ."

Edith Motte Young, recording secretary at the time of the founding, recalls how persistently the girls worked at living up to this purpose: Delta girls could be counted on for their high moral standards and their decorum. Osceola McCarthy Adams says, "There were, of course, many differences of opinion and conflicting notions as to how things should be done; but regarding matters of principle and ideal, there was a rare degree of unanimity."

The Howard University Journal of February 11, 1916, gives proof of the high standard of scholarship set by the Delta Founders. In this issue of the *Journal* there is a chart listing the joint scholarship averages for each fraternal organization for the previous four semesters. For each semester Delta headed the sorority list. Jimmie

Bugg Middleton remembers that Delta girls almost always remained at the top of the University's honor roll, and quite often won the prize for scholarship donated for several years by Alpha Kappa Alpha Sorority.

But morality and scholarship were not the only aims of the Founders, who were a spirited group, anxious to prove their value. As has been noted before, it would have been virtually impossible for Alpha Chapter, situated as it was in the nation's capital, to escape the influence of the then-flourishing feminist movement. Mrs. Middleton remembers that a Mrs. LaFolliette, an ardent suffragette, delivered a stirring address to the Deltas about how they, as Negro women, had a dual reason for demanding the ballot.

Shortly thereafter, in March, 1913, when a huge feminist demonstration was staged in Washington, there marched in the giant parade a group of Howard undergraduates under the banner of Delta Sigma Theta Sorority. Oddly enough they were led by a man, because students were not permitted off campus without a chaperon, and Mr. Montgomery Gregory, a teacher at the university, was the only one who could be persuaded to accompany the group. The Founders remember that for all their serious intent, the demonstration was something of a lark for the girls. It meant being off campus amid the hue and cry of the suffragettes.

But the home front for the Founders' feminist activity was the campus. Eliza Shippen relates that, as positions in campus life were opened to women, Delta girls were always in the vanguard of those seeking to fill them. But, the interest of the Delta Founders in equal rights for women was understandably subordinate to their interest in equal rights for Negroes. An early handbook, which includes a brief summary of the sorority and its intentions, states that the founders envisioned an organization "for concerted action in removing the handicaps under which we as women and as members of a minority race labor, and for promoting social and race betterment." Although the Founders were obviously limited in their capacity for carrying out such a large purpose and could give only token service toward this end, it was a seedling idea, singularly prophetic of what the sorority was to accomplish in the years to come.

Florence L. Toms remembers some of the Founders' initial efforts toward "social and race betterment." The sorority "adopted" the children's ward at Freedmen's Hospital, and the Deltas spent much of their leisure time cheering the sick youngsters. Time was given also to making nightgowns for the adult patients at the same hospital.

But it must be pointed out that for all their serious purposes, the group was composed of very young women who were, as one Founder smilingly remembers, "frisky and boy-conscious." Thus, while many efforts were made toward advancing lofty aims, much time was devoted to the purely social. The Delta Founders learned to shine as hostesses. Actually, Delta Sigma Theta remained for two decades very much a social organization, a large percentage of whose funds was spent on elaborate dances, sumptuous banquets, and so on. Yet the seeds for service were being sown.

3 *The sapling grows*

Organizing and expanding

THE FIRST FIVE CHAPTERS OF DELTA

Madree Penn (White) was a young woman endowed with some noteworthy characteristics, who was no doubt as important an influence on the campus as she was in the sorority, for she was the first woman to hold an office in a student activity at Howard University. She was the first woman editor of the campus paper, *The Howard University Journal*. At any rate, she was remarkable for the zeal with which she carried out an idea, once conceived. As the second president of Alpha Chapter, she immediately began setting the wheels in motion for the creation of other chapters. She had held from the first that a true sorority has several links in its chain; so she began an extensive correspondence with Ruby Martin, a young student at Wilberforce University located a few miles from Xenia, Ohio.

Wilberforce University, established in 1855, was a denominational institution supported by the African Methodist Episcopal

Church, with an honorable history. Among its graduates were many leaders for Negroes after the Civil War. Alpha Chapter felt it a fitting setting for its first offshoot. Madree's letters to Ruby about the new sorority were evidently quite inspiring, for soon Ruby wrote that she had ready a group of suitable young women at Wilberforce who wanted to join.

Now there was a problem. Alpha Chapter at Howard University was willing to authorize the creation of the Ohio group, but regulations required that an already active member conduct the intiation ceremonies, and circumstances did not permit an Alpha member to make a visit to the Midwest. It was a year later when Frances Gunner, an Alpha member chosen to represent Howard University at a student conference held in Atlanta, Georgia, met Ruby Martin at the same conference. Authorized by Alpha Chapter, Frances conducted private initiation rites for Ruby and instructed her in procedure for establishing Beta Chapter upon her return to Ohio.

On her return to Wilberforce, on February 5, 1914, Ruby Martin set up Beta Chapter. The new chapter was comprised of Ruby Martin, Annie Singleton (Newhouse), Margaret Glass, Bernice Sander, Helen Ferguson, Beatrice Mason, Freddie Billings, Nakomis Boyd, Marie Ody (Cobb), and Iolyn Springfield (Clark). Following Alpha's example, prominent women of the Midwest were named honorary members.

If possible, Beta set standards for itself even more rigid than those followed by Alpha. With regard to the selection of future members, they set a policy that it was not enough for the sorors to approve a candidate; the name of the candidate must be submitted to the entire faculty at Wilberforce for approval. Further, those candidates were judged not only by their academic performance, but also by their social standing on the campus, a standard that had never been verbalized by Alpha Chapter.

It is perhaps understandable that Beta's zeal in following Delta principles was even more ardent than Alpha's. Alpha had granted its new sister full equality without trial or probationary period, and Beta felt an obligation to live up to the trust. That Beta did well is proved by the fact that all chapters established subsequently were granted the same full equality immediately upon establishment. Beta has left its permanent mark on the sorority by its contribution of the "Beta Hymn," which is as traditional as the sisterhood.

Having made the venture toward expansion, Delta Sigma Theta now proceeded with caution. Continuous requests for permission to found new chapters came in from colleges in large cities, but it was 1918 before Alpha Chapter permitted another chapter to be formed.

The third chapter of Delta Sigma Theta was founded at the University of Pennsylvania, the first interracial campus to be penetrated. Some talented young women were selected to form Gamma Chapter, among them Sadie Tanner Moselle (Alexander), who was soon to be the first Negro woman in the United States to earn the degree of Doctor of Philosophy. The other charter members were Virginia M. Alexander, Julia Polk, Nellie Bright, Esther Butler, and Pauline Young. Mrs. Alice Dunbar Nelson, a talented writer and widow of the poet, Paul Lawrence Dunbar, was invited to honorary membership.

The formation of Beta and Gamma Chapters had been by the authorization of Alpha Chapter. But in the case of the creation of Delta Chapter, perhaps because of the proximity of location, the authorization came from Beta Chapter. Delta Chapter was established at the University of Iowa on April 4, 1919, with these charter members: Helen Dameron Beshears, Mamie Diggs (Robertson), Harriette Alexander (Vines), Ola Calhoun (Morehead), Helen Lucas (Banks), Ada Hyde (Johnson), Violetta London (Fields), and Elizabeth Gross Green.

Delta Chapter was the second chapter of Delta Sigma Theta Sorority to be formed on an interracial campus, and its creation brought to the fore a new problem for the sorority. White fraternities and sororities were considered to have "arrived" when and if they could buy or build a fraternity or sorority house; the more pretentious and palatial the house, the higher the status of the particular fraternal organization. Delta Sigma Theta Sorority was aware that it would be many years before she could hope to compete in this respect with the older and larger national sororities. But there was a distinct need for a Delta House at the State University of Iowa.

In those days, although Negro students were accepted by interracial colleges and universities for matriculation, there was no such general acceptance when it came to lodging them in the dormitories. Negro students on such campuses usually were forced to seek lodging in such Negro homes as would cater to them, and more often than not, such homes were located a good distance from the campus, forcing the students to travel for long hours on trolleys and buses to get to school. Understandably, this was a deterrent to effective study habits. Moreover, the Negro student often had to pay excessively high rents for poor accommodations, sometimes sharing living quarters with other roomers whose backgrounds made them undesirable companions.

Delta Chapter at the University of Iowa was determined to solve the problem of its members, at least, by having a Delta House. But they were small in number and not financially able to carry the full burden of equipping and managing a house. However, when their need became known, the Iowa State Federation of Colored Women's Clubs, a humanitarian organization, came to their rescue. The sorority owes this group a debt of gratitude for its role in making possible the first Delta House.

Epsilon Chapter at Ohio State University in Columbus was established in November of 1919. This chapter also was authorized by Beta Chapter, but it is significant that this time Beta sought the approval of Alpha, Gamma, and Delta before coming to a decision. With increased expansion, the sorority was beginning to recognize the importance of uniformity of decisions and procedures, and the conference concerning the creation of Epsilon Chapter heralded central government for the organization.

The charter members of Epsilon chapter were Phila Ann McGillery (White), Catherine Thompson Alexander, Bernice N. Copeland, Fairy Shores Burrell, and Alberta Hanley. Epsilon Chapter is responsible for the official pledge pin of the sorority.

Delta Sigma Theta Sorority now had a total of five chapters in its rosters, but the benefits of increased numbers were accompanied by increased problems. In their separate locations, no chapter could be certain that it was working along uniform lines with the rest of its sisters. Beyond the fact that each chapter was careful to choose the cream of the undergraduate crop for membership, and to insist on high moral and scholastic standards, there was no proof that the sorority was a unified body, nor was there any recognized source of authority. A possible radical decision by any one chapter could injure the prospects of the whole. Six years after the founding of Delta Sigma Theta, the sorority convened for the urgent purpose of nationalizing under a central government.

THE FIRST NATIONAL CONVENTION

Alpha Chapter issued the call to the First National Convention, which assembled at Howard University on December 27, 1919, with Alpha, Gamma, and Epsilon Chapters represented. Beta's representative was absent because of a sudden death in her family, and Delta Chapter sent no representative because none of its members found it convenient to attend; but both notified the convention that they were willing to abide by its decisions. Sadie Tanner Moselle (Alexander) acted as chairman of the conference.

The plan to nationalize was put to a vote and duly adopted. Then the conference resolved itself into a committee to work out an appropriate constitution for the proposed national sisterhood, and to discuss problems involved in perfecting the organization; the committee also worked out a national program designed to assure uniformity of procedure. The group then declared itself in convention assembled, and spent the following three days creating the Grand Chapter of Delta Sigma Theta—the local chapters combined under a central government.

The First National Convention elected the following officers to the Grand Chapter: National President, Sadie T. M. Alexander of Gamma Chapter; Recording Secretary, Catherine Thompson (Alexander), Epsilon Chapter; Corresponding Secretary, Ann McCary (Dingle), Alpha Chapter; Treasurer, Virginia Alexander, Gamma Chapter; Journalist, Bernice N. Copeland, Epsilon Chapter; Custodian, Harriette Robinson, Alpha Chapter. The offices of Vice-President, Chaplain and Sergeant-at-arms were reserved for the Beta and Delta Chapters to fill, and these chapters later complied by electing as Vice-President, Geraldine Jackson of Beta Chapter; as Chaplain, Mildred Griffin (Dobson) of Delta Chapter; and as Sergeant-at-arms, Hazel Shaw (Maynard) of Delta Chapter.

With the creation of a Grand Chapter, Delta Sigma Theta had now come of age as a sorority.

THE FIRST NATIONAL PRESIDENT

Delta Sigma Theta Sorority has had good reason to be proud of its choice of Sadie T. M. Alexander as first National President, for through the years she has continually distinguished herself. The niece of the famous artist Henry O. Tanner, and the wife of Judge Raymond Pace Alexander, Mrs. Alexander can claim many "firsts." Having been the first Negro woman to be awarded the Doctor of Philosophy degree, she became in 1927 the first Negro woman to be admitted to the Pennsylvania Bar. She served as Assistant City Solicitor of Philadelphia from 1927 to 1930 and from 1934 to 1937. In 1947 she was chosen by President Harry S. Truman to serve on the President's Committee on Civil Rights, and was the only Negro woman to serve on this committee. She was the first woman to serve on the Bishop's Council of the African Methodist Episcopal Church as its official lawyer. Besides being Delta's first National President, she has been official legal adviser to the sorority for many years.

The first National President was so assiduous a worker for Delta

Sigma Theta that she was elected to office four times. When, at the Fifth Convention, she was asked to serve again, she had to decline because of increased obligations to her professional duties; but she had laid the groundwork for the national body, a groundwork that was to endure.

THE CONVENTION: DELTA'S YARDSTICK AND GUIDEPOST

From the beginning, in increasingly greater degree, the Delta Convention has functioned as both yardstick and guidepost to the sorority. Here is determined what the sorority has done, what it is doing, and what it needs to do. It is through gauging the pulse of chapter opinion at National Conventions that Grand Chapter is guided in policy-making. Although the character of conventions has changed over the years, the function of Delta Conventions has remained the same, and it is safe to say that this is one reason the sorority has managed to maintain stability through many periods of flux.

The first nine National Conventions can be viewed as a specific unit of interest for two reasons. In the first place, these conventions were held annually. The Tenth National Convention marked the beginning of Delta's policy of holding Biennial Conventions. Secondly, the nine annual conventions were devoted largely to Delta's internal affairs. Beginning with the Tenth Convention, there can be traced an increasing change in the character of Delta's convention agenda.

The Second Annual Convention was held at Wilberforce University, on December 28, 1920, with Beta Chapter acting as hostess. At this convention all eight chapters were represented, Zeta, Eta, and Theta Chapters having been formed on the campuses of the University of Cincinnati, Syracuse University, and Cornell University respectively. Several decisions important to the sorority were made at this meeting. The National President introduced the idea of observing a "May Week," a Delta-wide program to be held annually to stress "Higher Education for Negro Women." It was decided that during May Week each Delta chapter would conduct a program in its specific community to inspire the young people of that community to higher educational goals. The results of this program have been so gratifying through the years that May Week is now considered an integral part of Deltadom. The Second Annual Convention also resulted in the official journal of the sorority being named *The Delta,* and in the authorization of graduate chapters.

The Third National Convention met at the University of Pennsylvania in December of 1921, with Gamma Chapter as hostess. The results of this meeting were the establishment of a Housing Fund and a Sinking Fund, a definite procedure for the admission of associate members, a committee on Standards, a committee on Scholastic Grades, and the re-election of Sadie T. M. Alexander as National President.

A new Delta policy was set at the Fourth National Convention, held with Lambda Chapter at Chicago in December, 1922. With its increasing numbers, Delta now had a representative treasury at it disposal, and it was proposed that some of Delta's funds be used to aid promising young women who were financially unable to attend college. The sorority readily accepted this proposal, for it offered the members a chance to do something tangible in the way of race betterment, and also could provide a hitherto unexplored avenue for new membership. This convention created the Scholarship Award Fund and the College Tuition Fund, the former designed to help young women beginning their college education, and the latter to help other students complete higher training. Each chapter was taxed $50 annually to support the scholarship program, but this method was revised at the Fifth Convention when it was learned that chapter dues alone could not cover the proposed scholarships; and it was decided that, in addition to her chapter dues, each Delta member would pay $2 annually towards the scholarship funds.

An event for which the Fifth National Convention will always be remembered was the addition of Mrs. Mary McLeod Bethune to the list of honorary members. Already famous as the founder of Bethune-Cookman College at Daytona Beach, Florida, Mrs. Bethune was throughout her lifetime one of the best-known and best-loved women of America. She was awarded the Spingarn Medal in 1935, the Frances Drexel Medal in 1936, the Distinguished Service Medal in 1939, the Thomas Jefferson Award in 1941, and the first Youth City Award in 1942. She was the founder and the first president of the National Council of Negro Women and one of the first presidents of the National Association of Women's Clubs. She had been director of the National Business League, and president of the Florida State Teachers' Association. Two Presidents of the United States honored her with appointments—chief of the Minorities Division of the National Youth Administration, and member of the Civilian Defense Committee.

The Fifth Convention, held with Epsilon Chapter of Ohio State University, also saw the induction of a new National President. Sadie T. M. Alexander had declined to serve a fifth term and was succeeded by G. Dorothy Pelham.

At the Sixth National Convention, held in New York City in December of 1924, the sorority adopted the "National Delta Hymn," with words and music by Alice Dunbar Nelson and Florence C. Talbert.

The Seventh National Convention at Des Moines, Iowa, held in December, 1925, concerned itself with the nomenclature of chapters because chapter expansion had now reached the limits of the Greek alphabet. The Third Convention had thought to reserve the title Omega Chapter to the memory of Delta's departed sorors. But the 1925 Convention ruled that the name be given to the newly created chapter at Western Reserve University in Cleveland, Ohio, and that the memorial chapter be called Omega Omega. A system was devised for the naming of future chapters by using a combination of Greek letters. This convention also gave its sanction to the Regional Conference as a permanent institution because experiments with these conferences had met with great success.

The Eighth Convention at Cincinnati, Ohio, in December 1926, concerned itself chiefly with organizing its first drive on inactivity. Perhaps the greatest significance of this period is that in a dozen years the sorority had grown to the extent that there was need for such considerations as regional conferences and drives on inactivity.

The Ninth Convention held in December, 1927, at Washington, D.C., outlined the duties of Regional Directors and appointed a National Vigilance Committee. The appointment of this committee, designed as the sorority's political mouthpiece to do battle for racial justice, marks the beginning of the end of an era for Delta Sigma Theta. She had spent thirteen years in self-organization and establishment, and now she was sufficiently secure to begin to make her influence felt in the interest of the larger society. In the future her program would grow with her membership. And although her conventions would be half as frequent, since it was voted at the Ninth Convention that thenceforth they be held biennially, it was envisioned that they would be twice as meaningful.

THE DELTA TREE GROWS

At the creation of Grand Chapter in 1919 there were five chapters in Delta Sigma Theta Sorority. During the following decade, 1919-1929, forty-one new chapters were established. These chapters were in one of three categories: undergraduate, graduate, or mixed. Mixed chapters were authorized in instances where there were not sufficient members in one area to warrant separate undergraduate and graduate chapters. At this time there were three ways by which new chapters were being created: by young undergraduate women at accredited colleges and universities who of their own volition sought admission to the sorority; by Grand Chapter's bringing its influence to bear in certain desirable academic centers; and by graduates who had moved away from their initiating chapters and wanted to establish chapters in their new areas of residence.

The year 1929 saw Delta established in New England, the Middle Atlantic States, the Midwest, the Far West, and the Pacific Coast.

It is significant that during the twenties Delta's growth was mainly by the creation of new chapters on nationally famous interracial campuses, although the sorority itself had begun on an all-Negro campus. But it was important then that Delta be identified with only the most "reputable" colleges, for the body was still greatly prestige-conscious and anxious to symbolize the accepted "best" in scholastic standards. In the South the sorority had penetrated hardly at all. The majority of Southern colleges with Negro attendance were still unrecognized by Northern and Midwestern rating associations, and Delta was hesitant to recognize those state associations not considered of national importance.

There were at this time, however, three Delta chapters located in the deep South. But these chapters were established at private institutions—liberal arts Negro colleges that had long and honorable traditions. They were Atlanta University in Atlanta, Georgia; Fisk University in Nashville, Tennessee; and Talladega College at Talladega, Alabama. The fact that private Negro institutions in the South usually were accredited before state-supported ones emphasized the sharp disparity that existed between white and Negro public institutions. In this decade the only state-supported college at which Delta Sigma Theta saw fit to form a chapter was West Virginia State College at Institute, West Virginia.

AND GROWS

It has been stated before that the Tenth Convention was in many ways the beginning of a new era for Delta Sigma Theta. At this convention the matter of Delta's "exclusiveness" in the face of numerous requests for the formation of chapters in the South was brought into open scrutiny. Was the sorority justified in pursuing a policy of recognizing only accredited "A" colleges and universities? As a Negro sorority, should it not explore the reasons which prevented Negro institutions from full accreditation and make exception in such instances? Although action was postponed until the

Twelfth National Convention, the concern of the Tenth Convention paved the way for the relaxation of Delta's stringent entrance policies.

There were, of course, several factors which contributed to the failure of Southern Negro colleges to qualify as "A" institutions. Although Negro colleges in the South and Southwest followed the standard four-year curricula, there were other areas in which they were found to be sadly lacking by rating associations. The norm was set by white colleges and universities, and state-supported Negro institutions were rarely, if ever, comparable in physical plants, libraries, qualified faculties, appropriate salary scales, or normal student enrollment. It was not until the 1930's that any sizable number of Southern Negro colleges could merit full accreditation. And there is some indication that even when merited the accreditation was delayed because of racial discrimination on the part of the state associations.

In view of the facts, it was only a matter of time before Grand Chapter would have to make some amendments in its admitting policies in favor of the Southern institutions. Many Delta women, graduated from Eastern and Midwestern colleges, had returned to the South to teach, and they were pushing the issue. Each National Convention saw an increased number of petitions for establishment of chapters in the South. It is also possible that the period itself was of some influence in deciding the issue. This was the beginning of an era generally known as the Southern Negro Renaissance. Negro leadership, hitherto usually derived from the East and Middle West, was now beginning to emerge in the South. The Southern Negro populace, which previously could have been dismissed as largely sharecropper and field hand, was now producing professional men and women and pioneers in the business world at a surprising speed; and the Southern colleges and universities were incubators and havens for the newborn literary movement of the decade which gave voice to the plight of the Southern Negro. In its search for women with the qualities of leadership and service, Delta Sigma Theta could no longer ignore the South. In 1933 the Twelfth National Convention ruled,

> that all colleges or universities rated "B" by any of the recognized accrediting agencies will be accepted, provided they fulfill all the standard requirements laid down by such agencies except those pertaining to salaries and training of faculty.

AND HAS GROWING PAINS

It would be unfair to give the impression that during these years of Delta's rapid growth and expansion, all was sweetness and light. To the contrary, the records show that practically every landmark in Delta's progress has been the product of much and often violent controversy. The organization considers this healthy. It is to be expected that women with a high degree of intelligence and initiative occasionally will find themselves at odds with each other. The convention, while providing a means by which a representative may contribute to the good of all, also provides a means for one to move into the spotlight; and the minutes are laced with amusing examples of members taking full advantage of parliamentary rules to lengthen their "moment in the sun." Because of this some conventions seemed to have been overly concerned with trifles.

As the sorority grew in numbers and resources, there was often a good deal of quibbling about expenditures. The truth is that Delta still had much to learn about establishing her finances on a sound basis. Only after certain funds had been absconded was the precaution taken of bonding the sorority secretary and treasurer. Rules for the receipt and disbursement of funds apparently were made as the occasion arose, and personal loans were made to sorors merely on the promise that the loans would be repaid. While this was evidence of an almost naïve sisterly confidence, default on the part of some of the borrowers was proof that the sorority could no longer operate as a small community—it was now a national organization and must perform as such.

Another result of rapid expansion was the necessary creation of new offices, and the inevitable dissent concerning those elected to fill them. The convention floor was often the scene of stinging attacks on a Grand Chapter officer who, because she was new in the position, had made some error in judgment. It is a tribute to the quality of Deltas through the years that in each instance, calm and reasonable decisions have finally been made, and that under attack most Delta officials have viewed the situation objectively and have continued to serve to the best of their abilities.

It is also a tribute to Delta that what she represents is so meaningful to her members that despite all differences her basic unity of spirit has been maintained. It is fair to say that whenever a need or a problem has been recognized, Delta has faced it squarely and found the means to a solution. The ruling of the Twelfth Convention was a victory won after strenuous debates through three conventions; and it was, in a way, Delta's first coming-to-grips with the idea of change. By making concessions in her standards of scholarship, she was changing from an aristrocracy to a democracy. Her ranks would now be enlarged with students and graduates of teacher-training colleges, where before she had boasted a membership of only liberal arts students and graduates, and she would no longer be distinguished chiefly by having as members the daughters of first and fashionable families. But with the foresight of her founders she knew that progress is dependent upon willingness to broaden horizons. With her decision to accept the change in her standards of admission, Delta Sigma Theta was expressing her will to survive.

4 *Flings wide its branches*

Becoming an instrument of public service

CHANGES AND CHALLENGES

The Tenth National Convention, held at Pittsburgh, Pennsylvania, in December of 1929, marked the beginning of a new era for Delta Sigma Theta; and it came at a time that was also the beginning of a new and difficult era for the entire country, for the 1920s had seen a social revolution in the United States. Throughout the decade, youth had thrown off the restrictions of traditional society, and the prevailing mood in manners, speech, and dress was one of almost hysterical gaiety. Fraternal organizations in general reflected the tenor of the times, and Delta was particularly noted for her lavish social affairs, her extravagant balls and banquets. Although Grand Chapter was diligent in carrying out the sorority's program of social and political action, the local chapters devoted little effort in these areas. Having paid their dues to Grand Chapter, they felt themselves free to do as they pleased. In general, much more money was spent by the chapters on local entertainment than in promoting the goals of the National Program. The change that was to take place in the 1930s was due as much to changes on the national scene as to the guidance of Grand Chapter. The Ninth Convention was held in 1927, and when the body reconvened in 1929, it met at a time when the nation was tottering on the brink of a major economic depression. By the Eleventh National Convention, held at Fisk University in Nashville, Tennessee, in December of 1931, the sorority had adopted a more sober outlook. In keeping with the needs of the nation, Delta's tinseled twenties were yielding to the thoughtful thirties.

Possibly the most hard hit by the Depression were the Negroes of the United States. As usual "the last hired and the first fired," the Negro laborer and his family were sorely in need of help. Once this was evident, the local chapters of Delta Sigma Theta proceeded to implement projects to aid the needy. The need was pressing and thus eliminated the need for motivation on the part of Grand Chapter. The local chapters gave baskets of food to the poor, provided clothes for needy families, and solicited funds and rummage articles for the less fortunate. Special help was given to the aged who found Delta's "Golden Agers Parties" a lift to the spirits as well as a source of needed supplies.

The local chapters also catered to the social and nutritional needs of children. Working through Parent-Teacher Associations, Delta chapters helped establish nursery schools, often paying the salary of a worker. In the belief that the children should least feel the brunt of the nation's desperation, equipment was purchased for playgrounds, community parties were given for the underprivileged, and many excursions and picnics were sponsored by Delta chapters. A large percentage of chapter funds was spent to provide milk for the undernourished.

Negro hospitals during this period suffered from lack of sufficient beds, linens, and equipment. Delta chapters responded to the need, often by equipping entire rooms. In many a Negro hospital bronze plaques testified to the fact that a room was equipped by a certain chapter of Delta Sigma Theta.

Wholehearted as were the efforts of Delta chapters to alleviate the distress of the needy, they dealt solely with the effects of the nation-wide unemployment. When the newly elected President of the United States began to implement his bold New Deal, the sorority had a chance to deal with causes. In keeping wih Franklin D. Roosevelt's program, there was organized in Washington, D.C. a group called the Joint Committee on National Recovery, designed to ensure that Negroes had fair access to the newly created government jobs. On this biracial committee, four Negro fraternal organizations were represented, and Delta Sigma Theta was one of the four. The committee devoted itself to exploring job possibilities and to assuring just placement in them for Negroes. Esther Popel Shaw was Delta's representative on the committee, and the sorority contributed large sums of money toward the work of this effective agency.

As the Depression began to yield to a gradual improvement in national economics under Roosevelt's New Deal, Delta Sigma Theta discovered that its own outlook had undergone enormous changes. Its concern for "status" had given way to a much deeper concern for human welfare and human rights. The bitter experiences of the Depression years had provided the impetus needed to prompt the sorority to greater efforts in the realization of her ideals. Much mention is made in Delta publications of the period of a "New Deal for Delta."

There are interesting similarities in the growth of all democratic societies, however large or small. In no instance can it be observed that the democratic ideal or any ideal once set is accompanied by a simultaneous perfection of practice. It would seem that the concept is grasped long before the full capacity for promoting the concept is acquired. Our nation, which from its inception has fully understood itself as a democratic institution, has labored through many centuries and will probably continue to labor through many more to realize its ideal. For democracy is continually shaped by its purpose to its purpose.

Delta Sigma Theta, who at birth envisioned her function as one of service to her members and her society, has followed a similar pattern. The progress which has been made by the organization in realizing her goals as an instrument of public service has been the product of the pressures of internal and external challenge. The development of a concrete initial program of public service to which both Grand and local chapters were dedicated resulted from such pressures and was a process which took some three decades. By the end of this period it could be observed that Delta Sigma Theta had created four specific and effective national projects in response to the educational, political, and economic needs of the society in which she existed. These projects, in full swing by the forties, were concerned with Scholarship Aid, Vigilance and Public Affairs, Library Service, and Job Analysis and Opportunities. In tracing the development of these projects it can be seen that each was created in response to a specifically pressing need which afforded the sorority an avenue for fulfilling its purpose.

SCHOLARSHIP AID

In the first five years of her existence Delta saw to it that her purpose of establishing and maintaining "a high standard of scholarship among women" was carried out by the simple expedient of electing, almost exclusively, honor students to membership. As the society grew it was obvious that a less limited policy would have to be adopted. In 1919 at the First National Convention, definite scholastic requirements for entrance into the sorority were decided upon, and Grand Chapter was vested with power to approve the scholastic records of all prospective members.

By 1921 further expansion caused Grand Chapter to create two committees, one on Standards and one on Scholastic Grades. The latter was granted the power not only to approve scholastic records but also to encourage scholarship among Negro women in general. This committee brought to the 1922 Fourth National Convention some new problems for consideration: What would be the best ways to inspire Delta undergraduates to maintain their high scholastic averages? How could such young women be aided financially, if the need arose, so that they might continue their studies? What specific aid could be provided by Delta for its graduate members who had the ability and the desire to pursue advanced training in a given field? And, what inducements could Delta offer high-school girls with the necessary potential to go to college?

It was apparent that moral support in these areas was not enough, and Grand Chapter authorized two funds to meet the need. These were known as the National Scholarship Award Fund and the National Scholarship Loan Fund. As its name suggests, the Award Fund provided for outright gifts of modest sums of money to be given to deserving students on every level as an incentive to further high scholastic achievement. It is understandable that on the high-school level such awards were made in the hope of attracting these outstanding students to Delta in their college years. The Award Fund also contributed to foreign study, and with its help several sorors have done graduate work at European universities. The National Scholarship Loan Fund was used exclusively for aiding students who found it impossible to remain in school without financial assistance. This fund was reserved for the exclusive use of Delta women and was dispensed in larger amounts than was the Award Fund.

To maintain these funds Delta exacted a tax from each chapter, but later found it necessary to increase the revenue by taxing each soror. Although it is possible that every member of the sorority felt the financial strain of the Depression, Delta managed to maintain her scholarship aid program without interruption.

By the early forties the scholarship aid program had made great forward strides. An enlarged treasury provided for grants and loans often treble the amount given initially. In considering the amount to be granted, the Scholarship Board now took into consideration not only tuition fees, but also such factors as the cost of books and special fees. As the size of grants increased, the regulations governing them necessarily became more stringent. The sorority was learning to protect itself legally in money matters, for there had been some instances in which loans had not been repaid as promised or in which recipients of loans and awards had not attained the expected scholastic achievements. Still, the scholarship aid program was in the main proving itself a worthy facet of Delta program. Scholarship grants and loans have enabled women to distinguish themselves in medicine, education, law, dentistry, social work, human relations, religion, psychiatry, library science, music, and every phase of the arts.

Much of the credit for putting the scholarship aid program on a sound basis must go to Naomi Cherot, Chairman of the Scholarship Board from 1945 to 1950. Under her direction, the policies which now govern the dispensing of grants and awards were designed to protect the sorority and to assure the best possible use of the available funds.

Besides the general Scholarship Fund, there have been established other special award funds. One was established in 1944 to honor Julia Bumry Jones who had served in the thirties as columnist and feature writer, pursuits then rare for a woman, for the *Pittsburgh Courier,* a leading Negro weekly. The Julia Bumry Jones Award in journalism was established as an inducement to young women to venture into the field of journalism.

The Juliette Derricotte Award was named for a Delta trained in social work, who had left a brilliant record in that field. After she died in an automobile accident, Delta Sigma Theta established the award in her name at the University of Pittsburgh where there is a School of Social Work. The award is used exclusively for worthy Delta students who hope to pursue careers in this area.

In 1952, the sorority established a scholarship award at the New Delhi School of Social Work in New Delhi, India. The National President of Delta Sigma Theta, Dorothy I. Height, had served as guest professor at the University in 1951. She is a woman well trained and widely experienced in this area and she has served for some years on the National Staff of the Young Women's Christian Association of the United States. On her recommendation, Grand Chapter decided to use the proposed grant of $500 to allow

Hindu students to study at home where college fees are less expensive than in this country. It marked the first time that a grant had been made by Delta for students in a foreign country.

Delta's program of scholarship aid is not confined to Grand Chapter. Individual chapters carry on scholarship programs to serve worthy young women in their respective locales, and the amounts given annually by local chapters are considerable, often as much as $2,000. Although no official accounting is made of such money, it can safely be estimated that annual chapter scholarships combine to average an approximate $20,000. With Grand Chapter Awards annually averaging $10,000, it is estimated that Delta Sigma Theta provides some $30,000 each year towards the advancement of the education of countless young women. In recent years, seeking to make her revenue go as far as possible, Delta has invested a portion of her scholarship revenue with an agency known as The National Scholarship and Service Fund for Negro Students, which seeks out and aids outstanding high-school graduates who wish to enter interracial colleges.

VIGILANCE AND SOCIAL ACTION

The Delta creed requires of Deltas that they seek the advancement of their race, and that they do so "barring bitterness." The Delta initiate pledges herself to take an active interest in her country and to use her influence for the protection of the unfortunate and the weak. As an organization of Negro women, Delta's first concern in applying these ideals has been the plight of the American Negro. Wherever possible she has used her aggregate influence to aid the struggle for full citizenship for all members of the race. The opportunities have been numerous, for the sorority was born in an age in which inequalities existed in almost every area of human endeavor.

Few in number, the sorority at first confined her efforts to Delta women and Delta problems. But by 1927 Delta Sigma Theta had grown enough in size and strength to make a co-ordinate effort in the direction of human rights. It was then that President Ethel Calimese appointed a committee known as the National Vigilance Committee, which was designed as the mouthpiece of the body to do battle for racial justice, to decry attempts at un-American practices, to protect women and children, and to endorse the appointment of Negroes to policy-making government positions. The sorority maintained its national headquarters in Washington, D.C., and hence was in a key position to have access to Congressional happenings; and the Vigilance Committee, later known as the Public Affairs Committee, could thus make immediate reports to the body on any vital issue.

Delta Sigma Theta has always seen herself as an American society operating within the framework of the democratic ideal, and she has taken marked care never to jeopardize her position as such. Early minutes show immediate rejection from the convention floor of any action which bore even the suggestion of communism or any foreign ideology. This precaution has enabled Delta to be fearless in using the democratic processes for the desired goals. It would be impossible to discuss in this history every effort of the sorority in public affairs, but certain major accomplishments cannot be overlooked.

As has been mentioned earlier, a major concern following the Depression was fair inclusion of Negroes in the program of National Recovery, and for this purpose some public-spirited white and Negro citizens formed a Joint Committee on National Recovery. Delta Sigma Theta found the actions of this committee consonant with her own goals and was happy to accept membership, sending as representative Esther Shaw, the chairman of the Vigilance Committee. Delta's connection with the Joint Committee now increased her possibilities for being well informed on pertinent issues.

During its brief life, the National Recovery Administration operated largely by code-making; that is, it set up "codes of fair competition" authorized by Congress. The codes made provision for the abolition of child labor, the establishment of minimum wages, and the restriction of prices. On November 15, 1933 Delta's representative reported that the Joint Committee, at hearings in connection with the codes of some fifteen major industries, had presented briefs opposing any discrimination in setting wage standards for Negroes. Acting on this information, Delta's National Secretary recommended that every chapter register protests against the treatment of Negroes under the codes, and that they urge the appointment of a Negro representative on the Labor Advisory and the Consumer's Advisory Boards. Shortly thereafter the results of the efforts of the Joint Committee began to be seen when several adjustments were made in individual cases where Negroes had complained of unjust treatment, and when conditions in the garment and tobacco industries where Negroes were employed in large numbers began under pressure to improve—and Delta took justifiable pride in the fact that her funds and support had contributed in some measure to the change.

A major function of the Vigilance Committee was to express the joint opinion of the sorority as a Negro group, and the Delta archives contain innumerable records of correspondence through the years concerning the many and varied issues on which Delta has spoken. But the sorority has had no illusions about the weight of her opinion. In such an instance as her protest in 1930 to the mayor of Sherman, Texas, regarding a lynching that had taken place there, Delta knew that hers was merely a small voice in the wilderness. Yet this knowledge has never kept her from using her voice, for she has hoped that her example would inspire other voices until finally the clamor could not be ignored. In this hope she has taken a stand on many an issue which she knew at the time to be lost. As early as 1930 Delta was urging the passage of anti-lynch and anti-poll tax bills, and through the years she has advocated cloture of the filibuster, which has so effectively blocked passage of bills designed to assure the rights of minorities.

Delta Sigma Theta has used her voice for individual as well as collective causes. In 1930 she made a protest to the Secretary of the Navy when a Negro on the Ohio State University team was forbidden to participate in a football game between his college and the

United States Naval Academy. In her letter Delta denounced the action as "putting the sanction of the United States Government upon race discrimination." In the same year she protested against the segregated transportation facilities, which were used after World War One to take American mothers to France to see the graves of their sons lost in Flanders Field. In this, Delta's voice was only one of many who condemned the treatment of these mothers whose sons gave their lives to "make the world safe for democracy."

No issue has been considered by Delta to be too small for concern. The Vigilance Committee once wrote to a life insurance company demanding equitable treatment for Negroes, who were being charged higher premium rates on the predication that Negroes had a higher mortality rate. The Committee also expressed itself in the interest of academic freedom at Howard University, when a charge was brought against the institution that it permitted its teachers too much license in expressing opinions. The Vigilance Committee also used all possible moral persuasion to convince interracial universities that Negro college students should be granted lodging on their campuses. It is hard to say how important a factor such protests were, but by the late 1930s most interracial colleges had admitted Negroes to residence.

As an organization dedicated to scholarship, Delta Sigma Theta has maintained a special interest in legislation connected with education. In 1937 Congress was deliberating the Harrison-Black-Fletcher Bill for Federal Aid to Education. Although the bill was laudable in its suggested appropriation of funds to aid state-supported schools, it made no provision to safeguard such Negro schools from being defrauded of their share. Negroes feared that if these funds were turned over to the states without any definite stipulations that Negro schools were to receive equal shares, these schools would be treated as unfairly as they were in the distribution of purely state funds. Delta felt this issue was so vital that she urged every soror to make an individual protest. Numerous other organizations were doing the same and it is evident that the wave of public opinion had some effect, for the bill failed passage. In 1938 it was re-drafted to include safeguards for the education of Negro children, but the opposition now was able to score a negative victory by blocking passage of the amended bill.

In the following years Delta was to lend her support to bills concerned with desegregation in transportation facilities, the elimination of discrimination in Civil Service appointments, and practically every proposed legislative action which would ensure just treatment for the Negro American. During all her public affairs activities, the sorority has lent active support to organizations in whose objectives she has believed. In particular she has given support to the National Association for the Advancement of Colored People and the National Urban League. On political and economic matters the sorority has often welcomed the advice of the NAACP and the Urban League, and when necessary she has expressed her opinion to these two bodies. The NAACP, which for years has borne the burden of the Negro's legal battles, has been assured of Delta's co-operation, moral and financial. The same is true of the Urban League, an agency which promotes better employment opportunities for Negro youth and adults. Delta is particularly indebted to this latter agency for its invaluable help in Delta's Job Analysis and Job Opportunity Project.

The function of the Association for the Study of Negro Life and History is implicit in its name, and Delta holds a life membership in this organization whose work has done much to call attention to the history and contributions of the American Negro, to establish Negro History as a regular course in high schools and colleges, to eliminate objectionable stereotypes from textbooks and educational literature, and to establish the annual celebration of Negro History Week.

The Vigilance Committee, later known as the Public Affairs Committee, was not a permanent Delta institution. It was dispensed with entirely when the sorority decided that the same ends could be accomplished more effectively through affiliation with agencies designed specifically for the purpose of securing human rights. For many years such agencies were Delta's vehicles for social action, and were felt to be adequate. In 1962 however, the National Board made a reappraisal of the validity of Delta Sigma Theta's program of social action. It was agreed that in the light of Delta's increased womanpower and unified potential for valid contribution in this area, such a program was not fully implemented by affiliation with other organizations. Therefore, the Publications and Public Relations Committee of Delta Sigma Theta was authorized to form a Public Affairs Subcommittee, which would develop a program of Social Action and Education.

Consisting of three members, Theodora Daniel, Elizabeth Reeves, and Charlotte Lewis who serves as chairman, the committee prepared for the sorority an outline of its goals and the techniques through which these goals could be realized. The goals were carefully designed to cover every facet of the stated major objective: To Stimulate Social Action and Education of Chapters on Current Issues.

The seven specified goals are:

1. To develop an appreciation of Delta's potential for influence in the community and nation;
2. To increase knowledge of current national and local issues so that every Delta will be an informed and effective citizen and voter;
3. To encourage active participation in political activity;
4. To influence enactment of legislation, national and local, of particular interest to Negroes and women;
5. To maintain vigilance over action or inaction by local judicial and administrative agencies and officials;
6. To cultivate a person-to-person relationship with the community power structure;
7. To join volunteer leadership in civic and other Social Action organizations, including interracial groups.

Political involvement is no new concept for Delta Sigma Theta. The sorority, since her founding, has been in the forefront of social and political struggles. With Delta's growth in numbers and program, however, there has been the danger that such actions might become matters to be dealt with only on the executive level, rather than remaining the vital concern of every constituent Delta. To avoid this possibility, the Public Affairs Subcommittee works to integrate social action and education into the total program of the sorority so that every individual Delta, in accordance with her Delta oath, may be enabled as an informed and contributing citizen and voter to lift her voice on behalf of the "unfortunate and the weak."

LIBRARY SERVICE

In developing a program through which she could best serve her society, Delta Sigma Theta has made a consistent effort to discover and meet the greatest need in the light of her capacities. It is for this reason that her program has not been static. From time to time she has relinquished a project in favor of another which appeared to be more vital or whose interest she could serve more adequately. The Library Project is one that has survived to the present day, with some aspects of change, because there has been a continuous need in this area.

The National Delta Convention of 1937, held in Cleveland, Ohio, gave its official endorsement to the much discussed project of a traveling library. By this time Delta had organized a great many chapters in the South, and representatives from these chapters brought to the convention reports of the urgent need for books for Negro children in the South. The majority of Southern schools with Negro attendance suffered from lack of adequate libraries. Some schools had no libraries at all. Moreover, Negro children usually were barred from public libraries. In most instances, the few books allotted to the Negro schools were the outdated hand-me-downs from the white schools. Supplementary textbooks were rare. Although such local Negro agencies as the Parent-Teacher Associations did what they could to remedy the situation, the need was scarcely alleviated. Here was an opportunity for Delta to help raise the educational standards of underprivileged young Negroes.

Anne E. Duncan of Washington, D.C., served as the project

chairman from 1937 to 1950, after which Maude L. Watkins of New York City continued the work. The project got underway with the purchase of books by Grand Chapter with funds supplied by local chapters. The selection of books was not left to individual chapters because of the effort to avoid duplications and inappropriate choices, but each chapter was assessed the cost of ten books at an estimated $2.50 each, and each book bore the name of the contributing chapter. Twenty-five book-baskets with lock and key were bought by Grand Chapter to facilitate transportation of the books.

A major problem in starting the Traveling Library Project was deciding which areas to serve. In what areas were library services most lacking? How far apart were these areas? It was obvious that, although the need was widespread, Delta's activities would be limited to her capacity. There were other considerations. The local chapters would be responsible for the supervision and implementation of the project. Therefore, the selected area had to be accessible to chapters that were willing and able to serve. And having selected the area, there were other questions to be decided by the sorority: What were the general occupational fields in the area? What were the age groups? What types of books would be in accordance with the interest and knowledge of the children of that area?

Two Delta women, Mollie Houston Lee and Virginia Lacey Jones, were serving as librarians in the South, and they were willing to supervise the initial steps. It was decided that the project should begin in North Carolina, for Mollie Houston Lee, who was chosen to develop the project, had the necessary wide experience in that field. She had founded the Richard B. Harrison Library and served as City Supervisor of School Libraries in Raleigh, and taught Library Science at Atlanta University and North Carolina College in Durham. She also had directed a workshop for public librarians from North Carolina, South Carolina, and Virginia, organized the North Carolina Negro Library Association, and served on interracial city, county, and state library boards.

The collection of books and the distribution of book-baskets required organization and planning. Mrs. Lee urged Dr. Virginia Lacey Jones, Director of the School of Library Science at Atlanta, to permit the graduating students majoring in Library Science at the university to experiment in the formulation of plans for the Delta Book Project. The reports of these studies presented a variety of proposals and opinions, and many new areas for consideration were brought to fore. In the rural areas where the need for such a project was greatest there must be a safe central place in which to store the books; a simple process of registering would have to be worked out so that a patron would not find it a discouragement to borrowing a book; the easiest and cheapest means of transporting the books from one area to another had to be discovered; books should also be made available for adults who desired them and a portion of the books should be bought with this in view.

After consideration of all these factors, it was decided by Mollie Lee and Anne Duncan that schools should be the repository of the books; that the population of the towns in which the schools were located be not less than 1,000; that these towns be reasonably near the underprivileged areas; and that the principals and teachers of the schools be asked to accept responsibilty for the distribution of books in the areas. It was further decided that each school should be allowed six weeks with each basket and that the baskets would be rotated among the areas. The Delta chapter nearest the chosen area would undertake the first experiment. The working out of all these plans took much longer than had been expected. There was the further deterrent of World War Two, during which other Delta programs took precedence. And it was not until 1945 that the project actually went into operation.

The Library Project was started in Franklin County, North Carolina. Franklin County with seventeen one-teacher schools, eleven two-teacher schools, seven three-teacher schools, and three five-or-more-teacher schools was considered the most needy of North Carolina counties. The county seat, Franklinton, was little better off, having two one-teacher schools and five two-teacher schools for Negroes, operating for grades one through twelve.

There was a high public sentiment in favor of the project, and a large number of citizens were in attendance at the official ceremony which launched the project. During 1946 the project was to prove most successful. Teachers wrote their appreciation to Delta, often stating that the project had inspired the community to contribute additional books to the library.

In judging the merit of the project, Delta's highest criterion has been that people have been helped to help themselves. Her greatest pride in this first Library Project was that it kindled the fire of local responsibility. Four years after the project was launched the citizens of Louisburg in Franklin County were willing to finance a separate building as a library center. The modern equipment in the building was bought with funds raised through the efforts of the teachers of Louisburg. The library, called the Delta Sigma Theta Public Library, was dedicated at a ceremony on April 11, 1949, and the mayor of the city presented the library keys to the librarian, Mrs. Mildred McCullers. To express its appreciation of Franklin County's response to the project, Delta granted to the new Library an additional $500 to be spent solely on books. Franklin County had been made aware of ways in which its needs could be met and now was able to carry on alone.

The time had come for Delta to move the Library Project to a new area, and Georgia was chosen for Delta's next library efforts. In 1939 statistics showed that only some sixteen per cent of the Negro population in the state received library service. An area in western Georgia consisting of three counties—Harolson, Heard, and Carroll—was considered by the sorority as the most needy of her efforts. Delta Sigma Theta now was not, as in the case of North Carolina, moving into virgin soil as regards library efforts. The Georgia State Department of Education had already made some initial advances in the direction of providing library service for Negroes, and had begun to set up regional libraries for them. In the early forties the town of Carrollton, the county seat of Carroll, had built a library branch to service Negro readers. The branch was begun through the efforts of white and Negro citizens. By 1950 there were fourteen such regional libraries in Georgia, but there was much room for improvement in terms of wider service and more and better equipment.

Delta's decision to carry its library project to West Georgia rested in part on the prior efforts of its Atlanta Alumnae Chapter. In 1947 this chapter had contributed $500 for new books to the Negro Branch Library in Carrollton, and this action spurred the Negro leaders of the area to follow suit. In 1948 the West Georgia Regional Library Director reported to the chapter that all together $2,000 had been raised for the purchase of books. The efforts of the Atlanta Alumnae Chapter and the citizens of Carrollton were brought to the attention of the Georgia State Department, which by this motivation immediately tripled its own grant to the Carrollton Negro Branch.

By 1950 community and regional interest in the library program at Carrollton had reached a new high. A new and more adequate library building had been built as headquarters for service to Negroes in the area, and the collection of new books amounted to about 2,000. But there was still need for library materials, standard library furniture, such library aids as a film projector, and, most important of all, a means of extending the service to all rural schools in the region and to the most isolated rural homes. Delta's Grand Chapter decided to meet this last need.

Early in the days of the National Library Project, Delta Sigma Theta had made plans for the purchase of a bookmobile. It was reasoned that such a vehicle for transporting books in rural districts would eventually prove cheaper than the method of railway express that was being used, but wartime conditions prevented the purchase. It was planned that when it had been purchased the bookmobile would be sent to aid the North Carolina Project. But by 1950 when the purchase was made, the state of North Carolina had made a legislative appropriation to provide bookmobile service for the Negroes in every North Carolina county. Since there was no longer a need for it in North Carolina the question was: Where should the bookmobile be sent? There had to be some assurance of reciprocal responsibility and co-operation with local citizens. Delta's National President, Dorothy I. Height, knowing of the work of Atlanta's Alumnae Chapter, wrote to Dr. Virginia Lacey Jones asking whether the bookmobile could be useful to aid the library program being developed in certain Georgia counties. In her letter she asked whether it would be possible to obtain the co-operation of the State Library Commission, adding that ". . . By co-operation we mean assistance in terms of giving us space in which bookmobile would have headquarters, co-operation in helping establish the stops for service, and, of course, some degree of co-operation that would mean that in a period of two or three years after the bookmobile had operated on this demonstrated basis, the project might be taken over by the State Commission . . . for we hope to stimulate the proper officials to include service to Negroes as library service is extended."

Upon assurance that Carroll County was the ideal place in terms of need and readiness, the sorority decided that the bookmobile would be sent there to serve the Negroes of the West Georgia Regional Library Project.

On Sunday, August 13, 1950, the Delta Sigma Theta Bookmobile reached the King Street Library Branch in Carrollton, Georgia, where "open house" was held in celebration. On that same Sunday the sorority was starting its National Convention in Berkeley, California, and this convention formulated plans for the furtherance of the Library Project in Carrollton. The convention agreed that for a limited period the project should be considered a development program, and approved further allocation of money to aid the project. As a result, within the following years Delta had contributed to West Georgia's library program not only the Ford Vanette Bookmobile, but also $3,000 towards the books it contained, a motion-picture projector, and a new record player. The bookmobile proved so effective a means of reaching the rural communities that another county was included in its area of service shortly after it began working in West Georgia. For its efforts in this project, Delta received the 1954 American Library Association's American Library

Letter Award, given for the outstanding contribution of the year.

Dorothy Height, during her administration as Delta's National President, was remarkable for many things. In particular because she never allowed the outlook and program of the sorority to remain static. At the 1954 Convention she asked the Executive Board to consider the future role of Delta's National Projects. In response to this, a Library Evaluation Committee was appointed to investigate the effects of the Bookmobile Project in Georgia and to determine whether similar demonstration programs should be implemented by Grand Chapter in other areas.

Edith Foster, Director of the West Georgia Regional Library, undertook the initial responsibility for the Bookmobile Project, and herself drove the truck to the schools in the various West Georgia counties. Later Mr. Leroy Childs, a librarian, was secured for this role, and he proved more than adequate to the task. Arriving in each rural locale, he did much more than merely distribute books. For those adults and children who suffered lacks in reading skills, he showed films, conducted classes, and gave lectures, even on such unlikely subjects as "Superstition and Science." The housewives, even those who could not read, looked to him to bring sewing patterns and new knowledge from the larger world outside, for to them the bookmobile was an "educationmobile." Miss Foster, in describing this unforeseen development, said, "That bookmobile is a symbol of something vital in their lives. It takes Mr. Childs to them. He is symbolic of all the books in the truck. This is their way of using the bookmobile. . . ."

It was obvious that the success of the project was due in great part to Mr. Childs, for it was his dramatic work that had helped win the sorority the American Library Letter Award. Therefore, the Evaluation Committee recommended that a scholarship grant be made to Mr. Childs to enable him to finish his graduate studies at Atlanta University.

Another interesting fact was presented by the committee to the Executive Board. Teachers in rural areas in the counties served by the bookmobile were asked to check out in their own names and be responsible for the books for their pupils. The teachers, it seems, were most reluctant to take the responsibility simply because there were no locks on the closet doors to protect the books. The children clamored for the books so eagerly that school authorities were pressed, for the first time in history, to put locks on the doors.

Delta's Library Evaluation Committee recommended that the library demonstration project in Georgia be discontinued since it had more than fulfilled its purpose; and that the sorority, in good faith and in recognition of a continuing need, publicly announce that the bookmobile had demonstrated its purpose and was now a permanent gift to the community. These recommendations were enthusiastically received and accepted by the Executive Board in June of 1955.

On May 12, 1956 the sorority officially terminated its demonstration project in West Georgia. At an impressive ceremony at the King Street Library, in the presence of state officials and community benefactors of the bookmobile, the gratitude of the community was expressed to representative Deltas, and at this ceremony the $500 scholarship was presented to Mr. Childs.

A book-basket project, similar to the one carried out in North Carolina, had been undertaken by the sorority at Saint Helena Island, South Carolina, where Delta efforts had contributed to the creation of nine "library outposts" to serve the island community. On June 1, 1956, a ceremony in which Delta presented the final check toward the purchase of books and a bookmobile for that area, marked the end of Library Service as a national program initiated by Grand Chapter. In view of the rapid developments in extending library facilities throughout the country, the project committee agreed that national efforts might be placed in other more demanding areas of social welfare. Delta's activities had pointed the way, showing how Negro and white state library officials could work together for a common goal. It had proved what could be accomplished by a community once spurred into positive action. The project had proved so effective that several representatives from other parts of Georgia and even some from neighboring states had come to King Street Branch Library to observe methods of operation to report to their particular communities. Having pointed the way, Delta now decided that in the future its Library Program would operate only on the chapter level.*

JOB OPPORTUNITIES

The Detroit Convention of 1941 authorized a new Delta project known as Job Analysis and Job Opportunities for Negro Women. The project was suggested by Dorothy Height, then Executive Secretary of the Young Women's Christian Association in Washington, D.C. Her position had made her extremely aware of the problems in employment faced by Negro women. She believed that the sorority was in a position to do something to aid an equitable exposure of Negro women to Job Opportunities. In the summer of 1940 she was appointed by the Executive Board of Delta Sigma Theta to serve as chairman of the Job Analysis Commission and to work out a tentative general approach to the project to be presented to the 1941 Convention. At the same time, the Executive Board authorized the establishment of six experimental centers, one in each region, and stipulated that the results of their experiments be presented with Miss Height's report, in the hope that it would prove to the convention body that such a program was truly workable. Because this suggested project was more ambitious—in that it would present more and greater problems to be dealt with—than any previously attempted, it was foreseen that it would not be so readily accepted by the sorority.

Miss Height's report included four suggested objectives:

1. *To know the facts about Negro women workers.* Negroes frequently lag behind because of lack of necessary information. We need to know the available jobs in our communities and those doors of opportunity which must be opened to us. We need to know the conditions under which our women work.
2. *To have our workers comprehend their problems.* A thorough

* The chapter-implemented Library Program will be discussed in Chapter 8.

understanding of their problems is needed if Negro workers are to be prepared to act wisely and effectively in their behalf.

3. *To give guidance and encouragement.* Our younger women who are preparing for and seeking jobs need our support.
4. *To create intelligent public opinion.* No single program or group of programs can have significant results without strengthening public opinion, which supports our thesis that Negro women must have an equal opportunity for jobs.

The Job Analysis Commission made specific proposals for implementing the project. It was felt that the program should be considered a community-wide endeavor in which local chapters should strive to secure opportunities for jobs hitherto closed to Negro women; to promote increased representation of Negroes where openings existed; and to give guidance and encouragement towards the most efficient performance on the part of young women preparing for work, seeking work, and actually working. The project, as implemented by the local chapter, should develop from the specific needs of the individual community in the light of expert advice about job trends and opportunities. Therefore the first aspect of the program should be "know your community, know your race, and know the agencies within the community with which you may co-operate."

"Knowing the community" required that data be gathered regarding the major ways in which people in a community earned their living, the degree to which Negroes were employed in each field, and the jobs which at that time gave an indication of possibility for being opened to Negroes. "Knowing the race" meant appraising the skills and abilities of the Negroes in the community, and determining the number of trained Negroes currently unemployed or vocationally displaced. In the matter of co-operation with other agencies, the local chapter was advised to "make a list of the organizations at work in your community, determine their scope and function, and select those with which you will co-operate in working towards a common purpose."

It was also suggested by the Commission that individual chapters should approach such well-established organizations as local federations of women's clubs, benevolent societies, and churches, informing them of the purpose of the job analysis program and thus paving the way for their co-operation. The assistance of women in leadership positions in labor unions should also be obtained, and qualified guest speakers be secured to make public addresses on the subject of employment and job opportunities. The local chapter should do whatever possible to give aid and support to Negro business, and to encourage the establishment and development of new business, which would create new jobs for Negroes. It should support all legislation which would advance fair employment and better working conditions. And finally, all efforts should be given as wide publicity as could be achieved in the interest of furthering public awareness of the need for such effort.

As was foreseen, when the report was read to the 1941 Convention there was much hesitancy on the part of the body to accept it. After all, these were women most of whom were teachers and housewives with limited fields of accustomed activity.

Hitherto, action on socio-economic and political fronts had been implemented largely by Grand Chapter, as in the case of the program of Vigilance and Public Affairs. Or, as in the case of the Library Project, it had been a program not likely to draw much opposition from any element of the community. Now local chapters, many of them in the South, were being asked to undertake a program in their communities which might bring some censure from those opposed to fair employment of Negroes. Moreover, there was the uneasy feeling among many of the delegates that they were not equal to such a task. The report had been threaded with much technical terminology. Such terms as economic trends, analysis of trends, census reports, unemployment statistics, defense contracts, veterans' legislation and so on, although in themselves understandable, were not a part of their everyday vocabulary, and conjured up visions of specialized experts, which admittedly they were not. The very title of the project, Job Analysis and Job Opportunities, was enough to frighten them away from the idea.

Had National President Elsie Austin and the Executive Board not foreseen such an attitude, the project would probably have "died a-borning." It was the simple outlining of their individual experiments with the project by three of the pilot chapters which prompted the eventual adoption of the new program by the convention.

The first report was made by the Baltimore Alumnae Chapter. Deciding to begin their experiment by doing what was immediately possible, the members of this chapter had arranged a conference with Negro women employed in five industrial plants. This was wartime, and some of the women were employed in plants devoted to wartime productions. Most of the women's jobs were in areas requiring minimal skill and training. By being encouraged to talk freely, those interviewed made known some important facts. The conference revealed the type of employment open to Negroes in these industries, the degree of advancement permitted, inequalities in facilities and conveniences as compared with those offered white workers, and the degree of integration practiced in each industry. The study also showed that in many cases where jobs were open to Negroes, there were few qualified applicants to fill them.

The Baltimore Alumnae Chapter then proceeded to make a summary of this conference and to publish the findings. Letters were sent through schoolchildren to Negro families in the community, encouraging Negro women to register for certain defense classes which were being sponsored through the Y.W.C.A., and urging women thus qualified to apply for jobs in those positions open to them.

The delegate from the Chicago Chapter told of the chapter's efforts to help place young women just coming out of school in jobs for which they were qualified. The chapter had gathered and provided information about placement possibilities for these young women.

The Knoxville Alumnae Chapter had been more scientific in its approach to the problem. The members began by making a study of the population to discover the ratio of Negroes to whites and the areas of residence. With the aid of the Y.W.C.A., they made a survey of occupations in the community and a comparative study of placement in these jobs. The chapter made charts to describe their findings and wrote descriptions of the existing situations. They also explored the attitudes of employers in these industries. Having laid the groundwork, the chapter now felt better prepared to do something tangible with the project.

The reports of the chapters enabled the convention to see that the gathering of the necessary information was not an impossible task, and there followed lengthy discussion and exploration of possible ways and means along the same lines. The question then arose as to what should be done with the information once gathered; here was the crux of concern. Many members doubted their chapter's capacities for using the information gained to further the project. The National President then explained in detail how, at this point, a chapter undertaking the project would not be left to its own devices. Regional and national committees would be set up for the purpose of directing the individual chapters to the best avenues of action with regard to the particular situation. Thus assured, the convention adopted the organization of the project.

The Job Opportunities Program was now launched, although with some misgivings. It took some time for the sorority as a whole to grasp the vision of those who promoted the project—to understand that the necessary abilities and skills would be acquired, however slowly, as the willingness to attempt was translated into efforts. In attempts at social and economic improvement, work that is ever continuing, confidence would be gained with experience.

By the 1944 Wilberforce Convention, the sorority agreed that she was ready to move from the aspect of "job analysis" into more practical application of the project. It was thought that the term "analysis" was too technical to describe the type of investigations which had been made; but in any event, the purpose of the project was not to confine itself to analysis, even should the term be used, but to secure action in preparing women for economic opportunities and to aid them in securing jobs. Therefore, it was agreed that the project would be known thenceforth as the Job Opportunities Project.

In the efforts to implement the project, a wide range of activities took place in local communities. Some chapters stressed child-care facilities for the children of working mothers. Although Grand Chapter saw such efforts as rather remote from the objectives of the projects, they were viewed as first steps in the right direction, and for this reason encouraged. More venturesome chapters worked in the area of training Negro women workers. Some used legislative processes to aid in the placement of workers. Throughout the country, willing Delta chapters were sponsoring forums, symposia, conferences, and public meetings to acquaint the public with the facts about job opportunities for Negroes.

In some respects the development of the Job Opportunities Program was made easier by the wartime conditions which existed at its beginning. The nation's manpower was occupied in the armed services, and some jobs were made available for the first time to women, and thus eventually to Negro women. But the cessation of hostilities in 1945 brought a recurrence of certain problems which had diminished. The National Job Opportunities Committee reported to the sorority that among the postwar jobless there were disproportionately large numbers of Negroes and that racial tensions in communities were now as forceful as they had been prior to the war. Therefore, the need for the project was greater than ever.

In the light of their immediate postwar findings, the National Committee prepared a kit of materials which included guides for action by the chapters, information about legislation for improving the working conditions of domestics, and a suggested bibliography of reading materials and visual aids. The committee stressed that there was no specific blueprint for the project of Job Opportunities, but that the kit was provided to make effective work possible.

Further instructions urged the local chapters to rely upon the advice of representatives of government agencies which deal with employment and so learn more about the government, whose representative would in turn learn more about Delta and the project; to hold hospitality hours for women in local communities to demonstrate interest and good will; to aid vocational guidance at the high-school level; to plan strategies for the interracial adjustment of Negro women who, for the first time, were placed in jobs with whites; and to disseminate information pertaining to loans, homes, and education for the Negro public.

In particular the chapters were urged to stress that it was not enough to place continuing emphasis on fair employment practices unless there was a corresponding degree of interest in better job-training on the part of Negroes. Discharged veterans should be encouraged to seek methods of improving themselves. Now, after its first years of often disorganized experimentation, Delta was evolving a vital and practical plan of operation. The year 1945 saw Delta chapters engaged in a concrete "Hold Your Job" campaign which stressed on-the-job improvement as insurance against dismissal. The results of this campaign proved the value of a central theme and of specific guidance by the National Committee. The project had survived its dubious welcome and was now a thriving part of Delta program. In the future it would take its place as one aspect of Delta's Five-Point Program.*

* See Chapter 8.

5 *The roots are secure*

Delta: a mature organization

COMING OF AGE

The Grand Chapter of Delta Sigma Theta was legally incorporated in 1930, under National President Anna R. Johnson (Julian). In the eleven years following the formation of Grand Chapter the sorority had grown to the extent that individual chapter charters were no longer feasible. The necessity for corporate existence was made clear when a group of young white men at a Midwestern university organized under the name Delta Sigma Theta. The Legal Adviser to the sorority, Sadie Alexander, notified these young men that they had chosen a name which had been used by the sorority for seventeen years, and so they obligingly relinquished it. To prevent similar incidents, the sorority immediately sought national incorporation in Washington, D.C.

In the Alpha Chapter Charter of Incorporation, drawn in 1913, the Founders had said that "the particular purpose and object of the said society shall be to establish and maintain a high standard of morality and scholarship among women generally . . ." The Grand Chapter, however, felt that the time had come to be more explicit in its statement of purpose. The new charter stated: "The principal purposes and aims of this organization shall be cultural, intellectual, and moral standards among its members and the members of its subordinate chapters, and to promote and encourage achievement in education, by granting scholarships and other assistance . . . to worthy and deserving members of its grand and subordinate chapters, to other individuals at its discretion . . ." The Charter granted the body the power to carry on its business and activities in the District of Columbia, throughout the United States and its dependencies, and elsewhere. The Charter of Incorporation is kept at the National Headquarters in Washington.

The incorporation of Grand Chapter was symbolic of Delta's coming of age as a mature organization. During the same general period much attention was devoted to putting the sorority on a sound organizational basis. The rapid growth of Delta during the twenties and thirties led to the awareness that efficient operation depends on efficient organization, and during this period both operation and structure were constantly being modified to ensure greater efficiency. In fact, every decade in Delta's history has brought changes in Delta structure and structural relationships to meet the demands of an enlarged membership and an expanding program. It would serve no practical purpose to explore here all the modifications in the sorority's structure during the past fifty years, thus this chapter is chiefly an examination of the structure as it exists today, presented as a topic of immediate interest and as a point of comparison for future records.

GRAND CHAPTER

The Grand Chapter of Delta Sigma Theta consists of every duly initiated member of the sorority who is financial and active, and those whose status in the sorority is honorary. Therefore, Grand Chapter is considered assembled at the National Conventions when all members are represented by delegates from their respective chapters. At the National Convention, Grand Chapter, by exercising its power to amend the Constitution and bylaws and to elect the officers of the Grand Chapter, controls the operation of the sorority. The formal actions of the National Convention are binding upon every officer, committee, and chapter of the sorority. Voting delegates of the Grand Chapter Convention are elected by active members of the undergraduate, mixed, and alumnae chapters of the sorority, and each delegate has a full vote at the convention. Inasmuch as the chapters select the delegates to the National Convention, it is the chapters which collectively determine the policy of the Grand Chapter.

By their power to elect national officers through their delegates to the National Convention, the chapters determine who shall act for the sorority as the Executive Board between Conventions. The Executive Board selected by the previous convention must report to the next convention through the National President of their stewardship, and the National Convention has the power to approve or disapprove their actions and thus determine the quality of their stewardship.

By this democratic process, Grand Chapter is the highest authority in the sorority; but the responsibility for the execution of Delta business and program is delegated to the Executive Board. Since the Executive Board derives its power from Grand Chapter, directions and edicts issuing from the Executive Board are considered to be directions and edicts from Grand Chapter.

THE EXECUTIVE BOARD

The Executive Board is composed of the officers elected by the National Convention and the chairmen of standing committees and commissions. This is the governing body of Delta Sigma Theta which acts upon the details of the program broadly outlined by the National Convention. It receives and acts upon the reports and recommendations of the standing committees. The Board receives recommendations from the regions and refers them to appropriate committees for study. It reviews the programs of the chapters and the regions to determine where the programs need strengthening, improving, and changing.

The Board, through the National President and the Personnel Committee, is responsible for the operation and maintenance of the National Headquarters and determines personnel policies for the staff of National Headquarters. It also has the power to recommend personnel policy changes to the National Convention.

The National President, as Delta's "Chief of State," is the Chairman of the National Convention and also of the Executive Board. It is her function to see that every step of all the processes represented by the structure is carried out, and she appoints all committees, unless otherwise provided. She is a voting member of the Scholarship and Standards Committee and an ex-efficio member of all other committees, standing and special, except the Nominating Committee. She is directly responsible for the operation of the National Headquarters and works directly with the Executive Director.

The First Vice-President serves as Chairman of the Scholarship and Standards Committee and is also required to perform all the duties of the National President in her absence or at her request. The office of the Second Vice-President was initiated at the Wilberforce Convention of 1944, when a group of pigtailed undergraduates protested that there was no undergraduate representation on the Board. It was the first time that the sorority was forced to realize that it was in danger of becoming alumnae-dominated. The outcome was the creation of the office of Undergraduate Coordinator, to be filled by an elected undergraduate whose function it would be to work with officers and chapters in strengthening undergraduate participation in the life of the sorority, and to serve as a member of the Scholarship and Standards Committee. Later the title was changed to Second Vice-President. The Second Vice-President is also called upon to preside and function as does any other Vice-President.

Other members of the Executive Board are the Secretary, who

acts as the recording officer of Grand Chapter, the Treasurer, who receives, deposits, records, and disburses funds, the Legal Adviser to the sorority, all Chairmen of Standing Committees, the Immediate Past President, and all Regional Directors. The Board meets annually at the call of the President and acts for Grand Chapter in the interim between National Conventions.

BOARDS AND COMMITTEES

Early in the history of Delta Sigma Theta it was recognized that the Executive Board would need help in directing all aspects of Delta Program. For peculiar needs, specific boards and committees have been created from time to time. Some have been Standing Committees, whose function is integral and continuous; others have been designed to serve temporary purposes and are called Special Committees. In recent years the sorority has taken pains to assure that only such committees are retained whose functions do not overlap, for there have been periods when the sorority was top-heavy with committees.

At present, Delta Sigma Theta has as its Standing Committees, Finance, National Projects, Personnel, Publications and Public Relations, and Scholarship and Standards. Among Special Committees there are Auditing, Convention, Credentials, and Nominating, the last three geared to meet specific convention needs. Many Special Committees which had been necessary were eliminated when the sorority secured a National Headquarters and a paid staff.

Delta Sigma Theta takes pride in its calculated economy of administrative units and the fact that these units all contribute to the smooth operation of the sorority's program; but this efficiency is a relatively new aspect of the sorority's administration, and developed as a result of careful and deliberate reorganization. Empowered by the California Convention of 1950, the National President and the Executive Board met at Vassar College in Poughkeepsie, New York, in August of 1951, for the specific purpose of seeing what could be done to put the entire Delta operation on a more efficient basis. The sorority had grown in numbers so rapidly that each year had brought new demands, and each new demand had been met simply by the creation of a new committee, so that eventually the boundaries of separate function were confused. The sorority was entangled in its own network of boards and committees. The Vassar Conference, sometimes called the "Streamlining Conference" or the "Mending Conference," was called to determine those essentials which should be continued in the organization, and to reorganize the basic structure of the sorority so that there would be no overlapping of function.

From the "Mending Conference," under National President Dorothy Height's guidance, came many new and significant changes. The Constitution Board was eliminated as a Standing Board, with the recommendation that a committee on the Constitution be appointed at intervals whenever revisions might be necessary. The functions, duties, and responsibilities of both the Judiciary and Standards Boards were to be absorbed by the Executive Board, except in instances where the former duties of the Standards Board would devolve upon the office of the First Vice-President. The office of Grand Historian was abolished with the recommendation that at a given time a designated person could be employed to write a history of the sorority. The functions of the Grand Journalist, the Jewelry Committee, and others were to be assigned to a new staff member, the Executive Director. The committees on Public Affairs, Public Welfare, and Public Relations were combined as the Public Relations Board. The Scholarship Committee absorbed some of the functions of the Standards Board and was re-named the Scholarship and Standards Committee.

The "Mending Conference" also proposed certain changes in policies related to the method of collection of fees. Perhaps most important, it recommended the official "family" of the sorority which is the present Executive Board, including only such offices as have a necessary function.

Many of the proposals of the Vassar Conference were unpopular at first with a large percentage of the sorority members. Some held that the elimination of so many boards and committees would accord a dangerous power to the Executive Board, now smaller in composition. The proposed changes were rejected by some merely on the grounds that they were too revolutionary. Yet, after eighteen months of arguments pro and con, when the report on reorganization was presented to the Cleveland Convention in December of 1952, it was accepted with only one dissenting vote. The wisdom of this decision has been proven in the years since in which the sorority has operated with far greater efficiency. Committees, each with distinct and separate functions, no longer find themselves at odds with each other, and Conventions, no longer having to be concerned with minor details, now contribute to a larger and more meaningful Delta program.

DELTA'S SEVEN REGIONS

The Regions are geographic subdivisions of Delta's Grand Chapter. The Region is the link between Grand Chapter and the local chapter; the chief officer in the Region is called the Regional Director.

For purposes of administrative efficiency, Delta divides the United States into seven geographic regions. These regions are termed Eastern (Connecticut, Delaware, the District of Columbia, Maryland, Massachusetts, New Jersey, New York, and Pennsylvania, and has 33 chapters), Southern (53 chapters in Alabama, Florida, Georgia, Mississippi, and Tennessee), Southwestern (44 chapters in Arkansas, Louisiana, and Texas), Farwestern (Arizona, California, Oregon, Washington, and Alaska, 15 chapters), Midwestern (Illinois, Indiana, Kentucky, Michigan, Ohio, West Virginia, and Wisconsin, with a total of 45 chapters), Central (Colorado, Iowa, Kansas, Missouri, Nebraska, and Oklahoma has 25 chapters), and South Atlantic (the newest and largest region has 55 chapters in Virginia, North Carolina, and South Carolina). There are two recently formed chapters which do not belong to any Region, those in Haiti, and Liberia. It is possible that if Delta continues her expansion beyond the borders of the continental

United States, there will one day be need for new Regions abroad. The National Convention may make recommendations directly to the Regions; but more usually recommendations to the Regions come from the Executive Board, acting on the authority of the National Convention.

The Regional Directors are full voting members of the Executive Board and carry the responsibility of interpreting to the Board the needs and resources of their Regions. The Regional Directors also are responsible for interpreting to their Regions the action of the Executive Board for new programs, policies, or procedures. Representation in the Regional Conferences is by chapters, thus giving chapters another channel through which to secure information about the sorority and its program, and giving the benefit of their local experiences to the entire sorority.

The Regions were established early in Delta Sigma Theta's history as a means for bringing the local chapter in closer touch with Grand Chapter. The Eastern, Midwestern, Farwestern, and Southern Regions were established in 1926, and the Southwestern and Central Regions in 1932; in 1960 the South Atlantic Region was created. From time to time, in the interest of geographical unity and sorority effectiveness, there have been changes of regional boundaries.

Regional Conferences are held in the years when Grand Chapter does not meet in Convention. Practically all chapters send delegates to these conferences, which are conducted by means of workshops, symposia, panels, and discussions. Here such items of chapter concern as membership, chapter meetings, rushing, pledging, probation, initiation, standards, and so on, are explored—concerns which could not be discussed adequately at a National Convention where National Program must take precedence.

The Regional Director has a key role in the sorority's operation. It is her responsibility to enforce the rules and regulations of the sorority within the Region and to administer discipline, to make recommendations to chapters and to Grand Chapter to advance the overall program of the sorority, to recommend and bear responsibility for the establishment of new chapters, and to plan and preside over all Regional Conferences. She must also carry on all official correspondence of the Region, publish minutes of meetings and regional conferences, direct regional and chapter activities, and interpret the national program to the chapters and help integrate it with theirs. Explaining the work and workings of Grand Chapter, she assists chapters in formulating their own programs.

Thus the Regional Director is administrator, secretary, supervisor, and co-ordinator. More than any Grand Chapter officer, the Regional Director comes face-to-face with chapter and individual personality problems. From her the sorority demands a high degree of qualification and excellence of performance, and therefore accords her much honor and respect.

THE LOCAL CHAPTER

The local chapter is the smallest component unit in the organizational structure of Delta Sigma Theta. As the route through which all Delta members, except those of honorary status, must come, the local chapter is the most important unit of the society. The national body can be no stronger than the chapters which support it, hence the local chapter is the grass roots and the strength of Delta Sigma Theta.

The local chapter has substantially the same roster of officers as Grand Chapter: President, Vice-President, Treasurer, Recording and Corresponding Secretaries. In addition, each chapter has a Program-Planning Committee and other committees for particular activities.

The President of a chapter of Delta Sigma Theta is more than a presiding officer. In addition to presiding at chapter meetings and conducting ritualistic services, the President of the chapter is responsible for appointing standing and special committees, calling special meetings, and for all communications from Grand Chapter. Material for the use of the chapter is sent from headquarters to the President, and she is responsible for distributing and interpreting it.

She is an ex-officio member of all committees, and it is her responsibility to co-ordinate the activities of all parts of the chapter.

The President works most closely with her Executive Committee. The Executive Committee is made up of all elected officers and the chairmen of standing committees. The Executive Committee is the President's cabinet, who are responsible for the business of the chapter. The President is chairman of the Executive Committee and it is she who prepares the agenda for executive meetings, while the entire committee prepares the agenda for the chapter meetings.

In undergraduate chapters, the Vice-President is also the Dean of Pledges. She solidifies the relationship between the Pyramids and their big sisters through her ability to interpret to both the pledges and the members of the sorority the relationship between the two. She helps the Pyramids plan the kind of program that makes the transition from pledge to full member natural and wholesome. While each member of the sorority is responsible for interpreting the meaning of membership in Delta Sigma Theta, it is the Vice-President who stands as a formal bridge between pledgeship and membership for the members of pledge club.

The Vice-President of an alumnae chapter is also concerned with membership. Her goal is the reclamation of all inactive members of the sorority. She works directly with the membership committee as it seeks to find ways to bring back into the organized life of Delta Sigma Theta all those women in the community who have been initiated into the sorority and who have drifted away for one reason or another. She also makes special efforts to see that the membership committee and the chapter give attention to the best means for integrating into the life of the chapter newly graduated members of the sorority.

The other officers of the local chapter conduct the business of the chapter in their several capacities, and in miniature reproduction of Grand Chapter, committees are designed to handle the various aspects of Delta program. All committees operate under the direction of the Executive Committee.

Delta Sigma Theta realizes that each of its chapters is unique according to its locale, composition, and capacity for contribution. The sorority, therefore, allows to each chapter a large flexibility in interpreting and implementing Delta program. A chapter in Georgia might implement a Job Opportunities Program with an entirely different approach from a chapter in New York. Grand Chapter's major insistence, therefore, is that each chapter do its utmost to aid the national project in each particular community in accordance with community needs and chapter capacity. The benefits of such a policy of chapter freedom are evident in the impressive record of individual chapter achievement in every phase of Delta program. Some of these individual chapter achievements will be presented in the chapter that deals with Delta's current five-point program.

DELTA'S NATIONAL HEADQUARTERS

A National Headquarters was one of Delta's dreams long before it became a fact. The subject was introduced as early as 1929 at the Eleventh National Convention, and through the succeeding years was constantly under discussion. Although the sorority was generally in favor of the idea, the dream did not become a reality until 1952. In the interim, the records show numerous "starts and stops" in the direction of obtaining a National Headquarters.

In August, 1952, decisive action was taken by the Executive Committee. It was agreed that a campaign be inaugurated to finance the headquarters which had been authorized as early as 1939 by the Fifteenth National Convention. It was further agreed that a financial drive be initiated to raise the necessary $50,000, and that Daisy E. Lampkin be asked to serve as Chairman of the National Headquarters Campaign. Gwendolyn H. Higgenbotham was to be asked to serve as Liaison Chairman of the Steering Committee for the drive, and a slogan was to be used in the campaign: "Every Delta in the Delta House"—meaning that every Delta, it was hoped, would contribute financially to the purchase.

Delta's appointment of Daisy Lampkin as chairman of the campaign was a wise move. She was a specialist in public relations and fund-raising; her long experience as Field Secretary to the NAACP and as an executive on the *Pittsburgh Courier,* a Negro weekly newspaper, made her the ideal person for this task. Hers was an impressive record of service in various capacities with many civic and service organizations. With Mrs. Lampkin spearheading the drive, by spring of 1953, when the purchase was made, the sorority had already raised some $31,000.

It had long been agreed that the headquarters should be located in Washington. The site chosen was 1814 M Street Northwest. On April 6, 1953, Delta's staff and their voluminous files moved into National Headquarters. Some renovation of the building was necessary, and the dual job of renovating the new headquarters and organizing Delta's files went on simultaneously. Mr. David R. Byrd, architect and designer, a graduate of Hampton Institute, had charge of the complete remodeling. The building has four floors, of which the first was rented until recently to assure Delta of a small but continuous income; but it is now needed for Delta work and storage purposes. The second floor is used as a reception and conference level, and the third and fourth floors are for operational purposes.

One of the immediate and welcome benefits of securing a National Headquarters was having at last a safe and central place in which to file Delta's innumerable records. Hitherto records had been kept, obligingly but inconveniently, in the homes of Delta's officers.

The purchase of the Delta building in 1953 coincided with the fortieth anniversary of the sorority's founding. Delta Sigma Theta announced to its members the celebration and dedication of the National Headquarters to coincide with Delta's May Week, the annual festival devoted to education. Delta women came from every part of the country to join the exciting round of dedicatory, educational, and social activities. The four-day celebration, May 9 to 12, included a reunion of the Founders at Howard University in a session termed "Delta in Retrospect."

A few of the highlights of this occasion bear mention. On Tuesday evening, May 12, Delta presented "America's Town Meeting of the Air," a coast-to-coast broadcast, which dealt with the vital subject, "Are We Losing Our Moral Courage?" The participants were Dr. Charles S. Johnson, President of Fisk University, who supported the affirmative side of the question, and Mr. Stanley High, Senior Editor of *The Reader's Digest,* who supported the negative. The discussion was moderated by Washington's well-known news reporter for the American Broadcasting Company, Mr. Gunner Back. By affording to the public the knowledge and ideas of these men, Delta Sigma Theta was pursuing her May Week goal—to stimulate and further education for "more effective citizenship."

Another highlight of the dedication of the National Headquarters and the Fortieth Anniversary May Week Celebration was Mrs. Dwight D. Eisenhower's reception at the White House for the members of Delta Sigma Theta. The First Lady shook hands with more than a hundred sorors and commented that the Delta women were among the prettiest she had received. Among those sorors present was Mary Church Terrell, who pleasantly recalled a former visit of hers to the White House when she accompanied Frederick Douglass on a visit to President Grover Cleveland. The visit to the White House was a fitting finale for both the historic anniversary and the May Week and Delta House celebrations.

Once begun, the project that had loomed so large in the minds of some Deltas, that of purchasing a National Headquarters, was quickly accomplished. In five short years after the drive was started, the sorority had raised the amount required to complete the purchase. In the spring of 1958 Delta held a Service of Thanksgiving at the Headquarters building and solemnly burned the mortgage.

The National Headquarters houses all official Delta records, provides office space for the National President when required, and affords space and facilities for the meeting of the Executive Board and other national committees, secretarial space and equipment, a focal point of operation, a clearing house for Delta activities on a national level, and a friendly meeting place for all Deltas.

THE HEADQUARTERS STAFF

From the year 1929, whenever the subject of purchasing a National Headquarters arose, there would also be a discussion of securing an Executive Secretary or Director; obviously, a national headquarters would require at least one paid employee to manage it. Because these twin ventures seemed to be inseparable, it is possible that much of the delay in buying the building was occasioned by a fairly wide rejection of the idea of employing an Executive Director. One National President listed the latter as "one of the most unfortunate steps we could take," further stating, "I have studied and observed the function of this office in two national organizations. It has provoked nothing but the most antagonistic struggle for control of the organizations with the Executive Secretary on one side and the National Officers on the other . . . An Executive Secretary is not the answer to Delta's administrative problems."

National President Elsie Austin was not alone in her belief that in creating the position of Executive Secretary, Delta would endanger her unity and well-being; for a long time this feeling was widespread in Delta. But Delta has been fortunate in choosing as leaders women capable not only of strong opinions but also of open-mindedness. Three years later, in 1941, Miss Austin was the one who initiated proceedings for the hiring of an Executive Secretary. In 1951, the "Mending Conference," under National President Dorothy Height, clearly defined the functions and duties of the new office; and at the 1952 Cleveland Convention, the recommendations of the "Mending Conference" were adopted. On February 1, 1953, Delta's first Executive Director assumed her duties.

Delta Sigma Theta is noted for never doing things by halves. Having finally become convinced of the need for a staff to conduct Delta business, there was hired not only an Executive Director, but also an Administrative Assistant, and shortly thereafter a Clerk Typist.

Patricia Robert Harris was Delta's first Executive Director. She came to the sorority office with a fine background of experience as a Y.W.C.A. staff member in Chicago, and as Assistant Director in the American Council on Human Rights. In her more than six years of efficient and enthusiastic service as Executive Director to Delta Sigma Theta, Mrs. Harris proved that her position was indispensable to the sorority. The first Administrative Assistant, Mrs. Letitia Johnson, was equally capable to her task, as was Mrs. Eunice Nelson, the Clerk Typist, who later served as Administrative Secretary, and who for her cheerful untiring service to the sorority was made an honorary member at the 1958 Convention. In the ensuing years, the titles accorded staff members were to change as were those who filled each position to be replaced.

With its continuous and rapid expansion, Delta has grown more and more aware of the need for peak efficiency in its business operations. Following the 1958 Convention, the Executive Board authorized a study of staff and Headquarters functions and operations with a view toward smoother operations, more productivity, and less expense. In June of 1959 a team of professors from the Business Vocational Department of Teachers College, Columbia University, was asked to conduct a study of Delta's Headquarters operations. Expanding program needs made evident the need for realignment of professional staff duties and responsibilities. Administrative and clerical demands on National Headquarters had increased over the years. The Columbia team submitted a detailed twenty-four-page report which the Board adopted; as an outcome, staff titles and functions were revised.

Headquarters Staff now consists of the Executive Director, the Associate Director, the Program Assistant, the Financial Secretary, a secretary, and a clerk. Miss Eloise Jones succeeded Mrs. Harris as Executive Director, and in 1960 was succeeded by Miss Marie Barksdale.

The Executive Director is the professionally trained administrator employed by the Executive Board to see to it that the policies, procedures, and actions of the National Convention and Executive

Board are carried out. The Executive Director works with the National President; she is an ex-officio member of the Executive Board and all administrative and program committees. It is her job to co-ordinate the activities and program of the sorority, to evaluate and make recommendations to the Executive Board for improvement of sorority structure and program, to be responsible for management of the National Office, to serve as Director of the National Convention, to see to it that Delta's membership, purpose, and program are given all desirable coverage in the press, and to supervise and administer Delta's funds.

The members of Delta's National Headquarters staff work as a team. Having clearly defined functions enables them to execute efficiently the business of the sorority. Considering the annual volume of sorority business in relation to the size of the staff, the smooth workings of National Headquarters is little short of wondrous. Every member of the sorority receives nine to twelve items directly from Headquarters each year—the financial card, nine editions of the *Newsletter,* two editions of the *Journal*—representing some 80,000 pieces of mail sent from National Headquarters to individual members. Besides this, special bulletins are sent to national officers and presidents of local chapters.

In addition, National Headquarters receives, processes and accounts for all money received by Grand Chapter; it works with all officers and committees in facilitating the execution of their tasks, and bears the responsibility for initiating new program ideas, for carrying out programs agreed upon by the sorority, and for working with other leadership, elected and appointed, to release the Delta potential.

DELTA'S PUBLICATIONS

Delta Sigma Theta's publications are major means by which the society preserves its unity. The *Constitution and By-Laws,* the *Grand Officers Handbook,* the *Official Handbook,* the *Pyramid Handbook,* the *Ritual,* and the *Delta Songbook* are all designed to ensure uniformity of procedure. With the exception of the *Songbook,* these are confidential organs.

For years Delta also published periodically an *Official Directory,* listing the entire active membership, and categorizing Grand Chapter officers, Executive Board members, national committee, regional officers, local chapter presidents, and local members. It listed not only names and addresses of all members, but also names of the institutions which they were attending or from which they had been graduated, and the current occupation, if any, of each graduate member.

Recommendations for amendments and revisions in Delta publications are made to the Executive Board by the Publications and Public Relations Committee. The *Official Directory* has caused this committee some concern because each year brings changes in name, address, and status of many members, and the expense involved prohibits frequent revision. Because the committee considered that the *Directory* serves a worth-while purpose, it has therefore been continued in modified form in each December issue of the *Journal,* listing founders, national officers, national committees, and all chapter presidents according to Regions.

The *Delta Newsletter,* a four-page publication issued monthly from September through May, presents to the members spot news, announcements, headquarters news, and items of special interest.

The *Delta Journal* is Delta's official magazine, issued semi-annually. This magazine was begun early in Delta's history and has undergone many changes in format and content. The *Journal* is not only the means by which Delta opinion is promoted and provoked; it is also the camera which records for future generations of Delta the development and progress of the sorority. Here are faithful records of Delta's thinking, Delta plans and programs, and Delta emphasis, through the years. A 1937 issue of the *Delta Journal* includes literary reviews, a playlet contributed by a soror, several poems by individual members, two pages picturing babies born to Delta women, and two pages devoted to crossword puzzles. On the more serious side there is a résumé of the life of Mary McLeod

Bethune, an article entitled, "The Chosen Few: Dare We Be Frontier Thinkers?" and a report on the Equitable Distribution of Federal Aid to Education.

This type of publication is in sharp contrast to the *Journals* of today. For the past ten years Delta *Journals* have been increasingly more concerned with Delta program as it relates to the society in which Delta exists. Current *Journals* usually are centered around such themes as "Windows on the World," "Delta Women in Government and Politics," "Human Rights—From Charter to Practice," "The Challenge of Changing Patterns," "Communications," and "Appraising Values,"—all indicative of the widened horizons of the sorority. Of the two annual editions of the *Journal,* one usually employs the theme of the coming National Convention, and this is explored by articles solicited from outstanding people in the particular field, within and without the sorority. The other edition contains reports from each region and the chapters within the region. The Associate Director is responsible, with advice from the Committee on Publications and Public Relations, for the editing and publishing of the *Delta Newsletter* and the *Delta Journal.*

INFERENCES

The advances made by Delta Sigma Theta toward establishing the sorority on a sound operational basis have been necessitated by Delta's expanding numbers and her expanding program. Her effectiveness in pursuing her goals depends upon the efficiency of her operation.

In viewing Delta's structure and operations, one important fact is made apparent: the sorority now realizes itself to be not only an organization dedicated to high ideals, but also a business through which these ideals are promulgated. There are those who occasionally bemoan the passing of the less regimented "good old days," of smaller membership and possibly of larger group sentiment, on the basis that there then existed a greater family intimacy. But, if this is true to any degree, it is also true that the present system, in its concern for developing individual and group potential for service, does more than ever before to attain the goals listed in Delta's Constitution: The fostering of high ideals in moral, social, and intellectual life.

6 *Heard is its singing*

Fun, fellowship, and fund-raising

THE LIGHTER SIDE

Every Greek-letter organization is designed primarily for fellowship, and Delta Sigma Theta is no exception. That her fellowship is devoted to service in no way prohibits her having a good time in the process. Since her founding period Delta has been noted for her gaiety, and now, as then, this is a major attraction to her ranks. Few undergraduates, if any, would be drawn to an organization with a wholly serious program. And Delta's social affairs are equally vital to the graduate member whose sources of community entertainment are limited—as in the South.

Knowing that the Delta spirit is highest at a Delta social function, the sorority has carefully worked out a program of activities for its members. No restrictions are placed upon the local chapter in planning its individual calendar as long as the activities are in good taste; but chapters are encouraged to develop also the activities that are purely Delta, such as the Jabberwock, Founders Day, and May Week Celebrations.

But Delta, being what she is, has a twin purpose in her gaiety. While she has fun "for the sake of having fun," she also has fun for the sake of Delta and Delta program. Most of Delta's entertainments are designed either to promote Delta ideals or to raise money for Delta program. As soon as the sorority began to realize itself as an organization devoted to public service there arose the need for funds with which to carry out the program. The larger the program, the greater the need became. The individual soror could not be taxed beyond her capacity to pay. Therefore, fund-raising became an important factor in Deltadom. At present, most of Delta's local income derives from affairs sponsored by local chapters.

Outside the area of specific Delta activities, Delta is proud that almost all chapters choose to integrate cultural activities with their social affairs. There has hardly been an outstanding Negro artist in music, dance, or drama who has not been presented in concert by some local chapter during the fifty years of the sorority's existence. In the realm of community relations there have been Mother-Daughter Teas and Luncheons, for which the Baltimore Graduate Chapter is famous. Many chapters regularly conduct book reviews, addresses, and other cultural meetings. In this way, Delta functions often serve four purposes: They provide entertainment for the members and the community; they contribute to the cultural enrichment of the community; they promote a climate of good will toward the sorority and its endeavors; and they provide an income whereby Delta may maintain her program.

THE JABBERWOCK

The Jabberwock is an activity peculiar to Delta Sigma Theta. The first Jabberwock was presented in 1925 in Boston, Massachusetts, by members of Iota Chapter. In an effort to find some new method of raising money for her chapter's scholarship fund, Marion Hope Conover of Iota Chapter conceived the idea of a variety show of a kind that would interest groups and individuals in producing skits, dances, and songs in competition for prizes for varying amounts. She called this new kind of show a "Jabberwock," a title taken from Lewis Carroll's tale, *Alice's Adventures in Wonderland*. The term is quite suitable for the variety of clever nonsense presented in a Delta Jabberwock.

The first Jabberwock was an immediate success, and the idea caught on with many other chapters of Delta Sigma Theta. Today the Jabberwock is considered a Delta institution, and many local communities eagerly anticipate the event. An important aspect of this innovation in entertainment is the friendly open rivalry it affords all Negro Greek-letter organizations—the chance to compete with each other in providing glittering light entertainment and at the same time co-operate for a worthy end. Other civic and social organizations are also encouraged to participate in the Jabberwock, thereby providing a showcase for the talents of each group.

Jabberwock funds are earmarked for scholarships to be given by the sponsoring chapter to young women of promise and ability, and for public service projects. Besides this, the Jabberwock offers encouragement and practical help to the development of any talent that groups or individuals may possess from pre-school to adult age-level.

Although the Jabberwock is an evening of sheer fun, much hard work goes into its planning and preparation. While each group is responsible for its own contributions, the local Delta chapter must ensure that the entertainment is kept at the highest possible level, and is responsible for organizing and co-ordinating the entire program; it is customary for the chapter to announce a central theme which will make for a general cohesiveness in presentation. Delta committees undertake responsibility for epilogues, prologues, music, backdrops and stage furnishing. In addition, a Jabberwock entails compiling programs, publicizing the event, placing advertisements, and distributing tickets.

Delta chapters know that their audiences expect a good show, therefore, much stress is laid on rehearsals, staging, and timing.

Judges for the awarding of prizes have to be most carefully selected in order to have impartial decisions rendered. All in all, a Jabberwock is a major undertaking, and is usually presented biennially rather than annually. It appears to be worth the trouble. Chapters have raised as much as $3,000 for scholarships at a single event. Therefore, most chapters at some time or another have produced a Jabberwock.

FOUNDERS DAY

Delta Sigma Theta records January 13th as her official Founders Day. On this date in 1913 the twenty-two Founders decided on the name Delta Sigma Theta; but the sorority does not demand that chapters conduct their celebrations on that specific date, although it is customary for chapters to observe the occasion on a day in January.

The celebration usually takes one of three forms: a public program with an invited speaker; a local chapter meeting, in the course of which a candle is lighted in honor of each of the Founders as their names are spoken in succession by designated sorors; or by a birthday celebration in which the candles on the cake symbolize the number of Founders. The first type of celebration is usually held by graduate chapters in community churches, while undergraduate chapters place the celebration on the college calendar of vesper or assembly programs. The public address need not concern itself specifically with the progress of the sorority, but may deal with the benefits of group organization as an instrument toward nobler thought and action. The latter two methods of celebrating are employed in closed affairs with only sorors participating. At such observances thoughtful re-dedication to the sorority vows is made, the sorors sometimes repeating the Delta Oath. With rare exception, all chapters of Delta Sigma Theta in some way observe Founders Day.

MAY WEEK CELEBRATION

The Second National Convention, held in 1920 at Wilberforce University, inaugurated the Delta Sigma Theta May Week. It was designed to give local chapters the opportunity to stress the program of "Higher Education for Negro Women." The ideas of setting aside a special period in the year for emphasizing the need and advantage of higher education for Negro youth was conceived by Delta's First National President, Sadie T. Alexander. The first May Week celebration was observed by the chapters in 1921. The slogan was "Invest in Education," and the sorority had printed thousands of tiny red and white stickers bearing this sentence; in the months following, these were to be seen on letters mailed from Deltas and on Delta automobiles.

The American Negro has long realized the power of education. To stand on equal footing with other citizens in this country he needs the tool of a sound education. With this tool he produces his leaders and the spokesmen who will fight for his cause. The need will not lessen even after he has attained his full citizenship under the law in every area of the nation; for, in that anticipated era, he will need even greater educational skills for the more competitive economic living. It is expected therefore, that the public popularity of Delta's May Week will continue. Since one of the cardinal purposes of the sorority is to foster scholarship among Negro women, the May Week celebration focuses attention in unique ways upon the necessity for higher education.

The celebration of May Week sometimes takes the form of a public program featuring an invited woman speaker who has gained distinction in her profession. She not only emphasizes the theme of education in her talk but is herself a living example of the program. Other forms of celebration for May Week are book reviews, plays, and cultural teas to honor women of renown. It is customary during this week for chapters to make their scholarship awards. Occasionally gifts of money are made to libraries and schools.

CONVENTION CAPERS

While individual chapters of Delta Sigma Theta often sponsor noteworthy extravaganzas, banquets, and balls, Delta's gayest social affairs are given by Grand Chapter during Convention Week. Delegates attending a Delta Convention make the effort to arrive well rested, because the week's activities allow little time for sleep. Besides the long and full daily sessions, every day brings its own exciting social event. A typical Convention Week includes a get-acquainted party, a tour of the convention city, an Artists' Recital, a Pan-Hellenic Dance to which all members of Greek-letter organizations in the city are invited, a Delta Ball for Deltas and their escorts only, a Delta Banquet, several cocktail hours and luncheons, besides other affairs given as a courtesy by other Greek-letter organizations. If this combination of work and play makes Delta Conventions exhausting, it also makes them memorable.

DELTA TOURS

In 1950, Delta Sigma Theta sponsored a new activity for its sorors. The National Convention was held in August of that year in Berkeley, California. The sorority arranged for a tour to be conducted from Chicago to the convention city, and after the convention for a return to Chicago by a different route. Deltas from many cities boarded the Delta-chartered train in Chicago and wound their way through Illinois, Minnesota, North Dakota, Montana, Washington, and Oregon to California, and saw Yellowstone National Park, Beartooth Lake, Mount Rainier, the beautiful monasteries in Oregon, the rivers, lakes, mountains, and plains which make America beautiful. After the convention, the tourists returned to Chicago by way of Mexico, Arizona, New Mexico, Texas, Oklahoma, and Missouri, tired but exhilarated by all they had seen and heard. The tour had been so successful that it was envisioned that Deltas periodically would make similar tours to other places.

At every National Convention, Delta sponsors tours of the

convention city, but a special tour such as the one just mentioned requires careful planning and programing. The 1950 tour was planned and supervised by a dynamic Delta, Alma M. Harlee.

The second major tour was conducted ten years later, in August of 1960, following the Chicago Convention. Deltas departed the convention city by plane this time for Jamaica, West Indies. Dr. Helen Richards, Director of the Southwest Region, acted as tour leader. For ten exotic days, Deltas explored the fascinating towns of Kingston, Ochos Rios, and Montego Bay, went moonlight swimming at Morgan's Harbour, sailed down the Rio Grande on a bamboo raft, watched the fishing boats come into harbor, and picnicked by the beaches under age-old trees.

Delta's most significant and historic tour was the African Study Tour, taken in July-August, 1962, as a Golden Anniversary event. On an itinerary including Senegal, Guinea, Liberia, Ghana, Nigeria, the Sudan, Kenya, Ethiopia, and Egypt, Deltas studied the ways and customs of these African nations, with particular interest in the role of African women in the various arenas of public life. Their findings, reported at the 1963 Convention, acted as further impetus to Delta's International Project.

It is possible that such tours will eventually be accepted as an integral part of Delta program, for they serve the purpose of not only providing pleasure for the participants, but also of enriching the cultural life of Delta women and broadening their horizons.

AND DELTA SINGS

Singing is one of Delta's dearest forms of expressing the Delta feeling and the Delta ideal. Whenever Deltas meet, Deltas sing. They sing at chapter meetings, at Delta ceremonies, and at Delta Conventions. They sing Delta songs and non-Delta songs. At conventions, a Delta choir is often organized to lead the singing. Those who don't sing sweetly, at least sing happily; but practice usually produces a fine harmony.

The sorority has its own songbook. In it is found the sorority's

National Hymn, a stirring song with words by Alice Dunbar-Nelson and music by Florence Talbert McCleave. Delta's *Sweetheart Song,* a simple and haunting melody was written by Eloise Penn with words by Alberta White.

The Delta Prayer, perhaps the most beautiful of Delta Songs, originated with Joanna M. Bush. The *Delta Mispah* and the *Delta Sweetheart Waltz* are also her compositions.

The Convention Program Packets which acquaint the delegates with convention proceedings often note that "This will be a singing convention. Be sure to bring your songbooks." The 1960 Convention featured the "live wires," a vivacious group of Grambling undergraduate Deltas who were responsible for much of the singing activities during the convention. This group served as sparks to flagging spirits. Conventions are mentally and physically tiring, and these singing breaks, planned at strategic intervals and led by the "live wires" made the 1960 Convention noticeably less so. In all probability, "live wire" groups will become a convention institution. It is safe to say that whatever shape or form Delta Sigma Theta assumes in the years to come, as long as Delta exists, Delta will sing.

CHRISTMAS WITH DELTA

For long years, the local chapters have, on their own individual initiative, celebrated the Christmas season. Many chapters have Christmas parties for underprivileged children; others raise money to give baskets of food to the poor. Some sponsor affairs to cheer the hospital shut-ins during this time.

In recent years, Grand Chapter, inspired by the example of local chapters, has also found ways of showing "goodwill to men," during this sacred and beloved season. But the efforts of the national body have been rooted in deeper social concerns than those peculiar to a community. In 1957, nine Negro children in Little Rock, Arkansas, under the direction of Mrs. Daisy Bates, then President of the local NAACP, sought entrance to the hitherto all-white state-supported Central High School. This attempt at desegregating a southern school in keeping with the 1954 Supreme Court Mandate caused an immediate and violent reaction on the part of the white citizens of Little Rock. Governor Orville Faubus commanded his national guard to keep out the nine children. Caught in the cross-fire, the Superintendent of schools temporarily closed the school. When it reopened the nine courageous boys and girls were again seeking admission to Central High School. This time the President of the United States intervened by sending Federal troops to protect the Negro children. For many months these boys and girls went to and from school under armed protection. They never wavered nor were absent and continued attending classes.

The Little Rock situation was so tense and dramatic that the eyes of all the world were centered on that locale. In spite of much sympathy for their cause, the Chrismas of 1957 threatened to be a bleak one for the nine students. At that time, uncertain as to the outcome, they were living in an atmosphere of constant tension. Delta Sigma Theta decided that it would make a concerted effort to express the sorority's sincere admiration for the valiant efforts and personal sacrifices of Mrs. Daisy Bates and the nine children to secure the right of equal educational opportunities regardless of race. An economic squeeze was being put on Mrs. Bates and her husband who owned and published a newspaper, the *Arkansas State Press*. Although the paper was eventually forced out of business, that Christmas eighty-three chapters of Delta bought advertising space in the *Arkansas State Press*. The chapters also contributed more than one hundred gifts and some $300 in cash to the children. More important than the material offerings was the moral and spiritual support offered to these few who were leading a fight that would be of benefit to all. Delta's Little Rock Christmas Party was also a recognition of Delta's responsibility and commitment to the democratic and orderly methods of achieving human rights for all people.

The Christmas of 1958 was marked by a different kind of Delta giving. Sympathetic with the plight of the numberless women in

Kenya, Africa, who received no care before, during, nor after the birth of their babies, Delta Sigma Theta began a drive to raise $5,000 for the equipment of a maternity wing at the Njorge Mungai Hospital. The drive was launched at a reception held in the Empire Room of New York's Waldorf-Astoria Hotel. Dr. Njorge Mungai, the director of the hospital, was present and made the acceptance speech. This followed an induction ceremony at which Miss Lena Horne, famous stage and screen star, was made an honorary member of the sorority. Miss Horne cut a ribbon revealing a replica of "The Delta Sigma Theta Sorority Maternity Wing of the Njorge Mungai Hospital."

At this event, Delta was celebrating its Christmas season by sending gifts abroad. But whether at home or abroad, contributing to the welfare of individuals or institutions through its annual Christmas Party is Delta's community-service way of sharing with others the spirit of Christmas.

The Christmas Party of 1959 was in some ways similar to that of 1957. The sorority sent money and gifts to Petersburg, Virginia, and at a party held there presented them to the 57 members of the "Lost Class of Prince Edward County High School." This "Lost Class" was the County School's senior class which had expected to graduate in May. But the 57 boys and girls were among the 1700 Negro pupils left school-less that year when county officials closed the public school rather than obey the 1954 Supreme Court ruling to desegregate. Highly critical of the injustice dealt these students, Delta gave the party to express appreciation of the valiant efforts and sacrifices of the children and parents.

The party was held at Gillfield Baptist Church in Petersburg, and many prominent people were present. Delta presented gifts to the children, and also scholarships to enable them to complete their studies elsewhere. In raising scholarship funds, Delta worked in conjunction with the National Council of Negro Women and with the Prince Edward County Christian Association, an organization formed specifically to meet the school crisis.

Delta's 1960 Christmas Party was given in New Orleans for the four six-year old girls who were the first to desegregate the elementary schools of that city. It was a gala affair to which some 300 guests, young and adult, were invited. Delta played a lavish Santa Claus, providing gifts for all the children present.

In 1961, Delta made its Christmas gift to 70 high school students in McComb, Mississippi. The youngsters were expelled from the public schools of McComb, after refusing to sign a pledge to discontinue their non-violent demonstrations in protest of the unwarranted dismissal from school and incarceration of a fifteen year old fellow student, Brenda Travis. The valiant young girl was arrested on August 30, 1961 as she sat in the Greyhound Bus Terminal in McComb with an interstate ticket, a volunteer Freedom Rider seeking to test the law providing for non-segregated interstate travel. Brenda was subsequently tried and confined at Oakley Training Schools for Delinquents.

At this Christmas Party, Delta chapters made contributions of over $3,600 towards a fund to enable the 70 students to finance their tuition and room and board fees at a private college in Jackson, Mississippi, that had opened its doors to provide high school facilities, and also to aid Brenda Travis.

In 1962, the Christmas Party was held in Albany, Georgia. The Negroes of that city had, during the year, been struggling with joint determination to secure their civil rights in many areas. By December 1962, more than 1,000 persons had been arrested in the Albany Movement. Often Albany Deltas were to be found in the vanguard of the struggle. An Albany Delta, Marion King, was knocked unconscious by the police after driving to Camilla, Georgia, to take food to the daughter of a friend, who along with more than 100 teenagers was incarcerated in Camilla for marching towards City Hall. Mrs. King had her three children with her, the three-year-old in her arms, when knocked to the ground and kicked in the head by an officer. She was six-months pregnant at the time, and subsequently lost the baby.

The Negroes of Albany were suffering severe economic reprisals for their efforts to desegregate public facilities and to increase voter registration. The 1962 Delta Christmas Party was held to provide clothing for children whose parents lost their jobs because of participating in the Albany Movement, and aiding the voter registration project.

The Christmas Party is now an established event in Delta program. Its nature will inevitably vary from year to year to meet the most pressing demand of the particular time; but foreseeably, its spirit will endure. For wherever there are forces at work to achieve freedom and dignity for all—where there are sacrifices made to relieve pain, oppression, or need, Delta is bound by her convictions to add her forces, her sacrifices, her gifts. Her Christmas Parties annually celebrate this determination.

REPRISE

Principles which apply to the individual are generally applicable to the group. As relaxation, creative and contributive self-expression, and the element of laughter are necessary to the development and balance of the individual, so are they necessary to the vitality of an organization. That Delta Sigma Theta often directs her amusements into serviceable channels in no way robs them of their capacity for giving pleasure. Most of her membership is relatively young, and the sorority expects and provides that youth be served. Therefore, however weighted with serious matters her program may be, the sorority strives to balance it with pleasurable social affairs.

This is a wisdom shared by all Negro fraternal organizations. Many such organizations are in some way devoted to service. This is true because of the very nature of the society in which they exist. Seldom do white fraternal organizations undertake a similar program for they exist in privileged ethnic groups and have little, or at least no continuing concern for social problems. But the Negro organization with its large and serious concerns has even greater need for amusement and relaxation. So it is that the American Council on Human Rights, an affiliation of Negro fraternal societies, employed this wisdom when it was once necessary to ask for sacrifices on the part of her affiliates of which Delta was one until 1962.

On March 24, 1960, ACHR issued a bulletin to its members asking their support for the students throughout the South who were protesting segregation at store-operated lunch counters by merely sitting down at the counters and waiting for the service which would not be forthcoming. Merely sitting down involved violent persecution by white bystanders and the eventual bookings by the police.

The presidents of the sororities which then comprised ACHR issued a joint bulletin to the membership: "We are asking our more than 1,000 chapters to relinquish plans for free formal functions until our rights are won. Over a half million dollars a year are spent by college-based groups on social functions. This money can be better utilized to fight for equality and human dignity and to support fully the peaceful demonstrations against racial discrimination and segregation." But such a hard edict bore softening. In some communities the particular function was *the* event of the year. While ACHR urged chapters all over the country to cancel free formal dances, at the same time it suggested that the function could be had if an admittance fee were charged and the proceeds sent to the Student Emergency Fund of ACHR. Funds so raised were used to pay fines and bails and to give legal aid to students arrested or injured because of peaceful protest demonstrations.

As a final concession to the membership's valid need for fun, ACHR added, "If you do not wish to cancel your formal function, match the dollars spent on the dance with the same number of dollars for the Student Emergency Fund."

The five sororities which then comprised ACHR rose to the challenge. When the response was estimated, Delta Sigma Theta was proud that she, like Abou Ben Adhem, led all the rest.

7 *In tune with its brothers*

Co-operating with other organizations

TOWARD REAL FRATERNITY

Several instances previously have been cited in which Delta Sigma Theta co-operated successfully for common aims with other organizations. The sorority shows a sound maturity in her willingness to co-operate with others in achieving her goals, but it is a maturity which had to be developed. Like most organizations of its kind, Delta Sigma Theta began with an attitude of fraternal clannishness. The understanding of the need for joining forces with other groups was developed in stages as Delta's program perspectives grew. The problems of collegiate life and, on broader levels, the problems of the community, the race, and the nation were common ones and were too big to be solved by a lone organization such as Delta.

Much of that of which Delta is proud has been achieved in co-operation with other agencies. In viewing the nature, the development and the scope of this co-operation, it will be noted that seldom are such connections extraneous to Delta program; in most instances the association is a natural development implicit in the demands of a particular project.

There are, at present, three types of organizations with which Delta co-operates in specific endeavors: Negro fraternal organizations; organizations designed specifically to aid the Negro; organizations designed for humanitarian purposes, regardless of race, creed, or color. Delta's affiliation with agencies of these types were developed in the same respective chronological order, and this fact is a simple index of the nature of the sorority's growth in thinking during her first half-century. From her first tentative steps toward associating with other Negro fraternal organizations, to association with other groups concerned with securing Negro rights, to the associations devoted to broader areas of society, Delta Sigma Theta has made a journey in understanding toward the real fraternity—a fraternity in which, while preserving their distinct identities, all groups of men consider themselves brothers.

DELTA CO-OPERATES WITH OTHER GREEKS

Negro fraternal organizations did not exist until the twentieth century, but most of them came into being within the first two decades of the century. There is some evidence that there was a measure of interfraternal co-operation before 1920. College literature of the decade beginning 1910 mentions interfraternal groups and interfraternal alliances, but these references are vague and do not constitute official records of any such groups.

As Negro fraternities and sororities increased in number and spread their chapters to all parts of the country, the necessity arose for a national interfraternal organization to co-ordinate college procedure affecting them. The first National Interfraternal Council composed of Negro groups met in Washington, D.C., April 17-19, 1922. Delegates to this meeting included at least one national officer and other members from the following groups, the only then existing Negro fraternities and sororities: Omega Psi Phi, Phi Beta Sigma, Alpha Phi Alpha, and Kappa Alpha Psi fraternities; and

Delta Sigma Theta, Alpha Kappa Alpha, and Zeta Phi Beta sororities. That each was represented proved their interest in forming an organization which would enable them to co-operate on common goals and campus procedures.

This first Interfraternal Council was organized for three major purposes: to establish uniform qualifications for all candidates seeking membership in any constituent group of the Council; to limit the initiating of graduate members to persons holding degrees from accredited schools on a list to be prepared by the Council; to make rules to the effect that fraternal groups abandon underhanded competition and insidious propaganda. The necessity for this last purpose was itself an indication of the need for the National Interfraternal Council.

The Council was understood from the beginning to be a temporary organization, an experiment in Negro interfraternal co-operation. The temporary council dissolved in 1924, having neither failed nor succeeded in its purpose, but having laid the groundwork for such co-operation.

After much planning in the ensuing years for a more permanent organization, the National Pan-Hellenic Council was formed in May, 1930. The purpose of the group as stated at the time was unanimity of thought and action as far as possible in the conduct of the Greek-letter collegiate fraternities and sororities, and consideration of problems of mutual interest to the member organization. It must be remembered that when the Pan-Hellenic Council was formed, all its member groups were comparatively young. And, typical of youth, there existed between them intense rivalries and often no small animosity. Thus their willingness to form an alliance was tinged with some suspicion and a measure of uncertainty, which accounts perhaps for the swift dissolution of the Interfraternal Council. That the succeeding Pan-Hellenic Council made direct and immediate plans and did not consider itself an experimental group is proof of six years of rapid growth toward better interfraternal relationships.

Anna Johnson Julian, then National President of Delta Sigma

Theta, was elected treasurer of NPHC. In her report to the Delta Biennial Convention of 1931, she said:

> The coming together of these organizations is a significant step in the history of Greek-letter societies. In the past all efforts have been thwarted. Such a step seems, however, the only intelligent one for an intelligent group. We learn to respect and understand each other when we can discuss our common problems on common ground.

In the succeeding years the National Pan-Hellenic Council devoted itself to achieving unanimity of thought and action on the part of its constituents. Delta gave its fullest co-operation here, for certain of the NPHC aims were of particular interest to the sorority. For example, recognition of standard colleges by the better-known rating associations, together with insistance upon high standards of scholarship for pledging prospective members, had been the sorority's pressing concern since the organization of Grand Chapter in 1919.

In 1937, the National Pan-Hellenic Council voted to incorporate and obtained a charter from the State of Illinois. With incorporation also came constitutional provisions whereby local Pan-Hellenic Councils might affiliate with the National Council and be represented at its annual meetings. Since 1937, NPHC's concern with standards and scholarships has been continuing and the Council has also implemented specific projects to aid in making the life of Negro people more meaningful. During World War Two the Council pressed for integration of Negroes into all branches of the armed services, the opening up of war jobs on the basis of ability, and the passage of progressive legislation; in recent years it has sought equal opportunities in education and labor for minorities, and developed a program of intercultural education.

Delta's second and more recent venture into the area of interfraternal effort began in 1948 when it was agreed that the sororitiy should lend its support to another joint program, that of the American Council on Human Rights. For ten years prior to the formation of the Council, Alpha Kappa Alpha Sorority had maintained as a national project its National Non-partisan Council in Washington, D.C. Through this vehicle AKA Sorority had made representation to Congress concerning issues of importance to Negro citizens, and had acquainted its own members of the necessity for grass-roots, non-partisan political action to achieve desired legislative goals.

Between 1946 and 1948, the leaders of AKA discussed with the heads of other Negro Greek-letter organizations the possibility of converting the Non-Partisan Council into a co-operative venture. Agreement to this proposal was reached by the groups in 1948, and with their collective endorsement the new organization was set up in Washington.

Delta Sigma Theta, in affiliating with the American Council on Human Rights, was expressing her understanding of the need for united efforts on the part of Negro groups in the areas of social and political action. As originally stated, the purpose of ACHR was, in essence, to study policy and legislation affecting civil rights, and to seek effective ways to express its opinion concerning them; and further, to seek to have enacted, administered, and enforced the laws effectuating the same.

Several of Delta's key women have represented the sorority on ACHR's Board of Directors: among them, Dorothy I. Height, Patricia R. Harris, Bertrell C. Wright, Mae W. Downs, and Charlotte R. Lewis.

There have often been questions in the minds of Deltas as to whether or not the sorority has scattered its public affairs energies by affiliating with too many organizations whose purpose is action for obtaining human rights. There being some evidence to support this concern, the Executive Board of Delta Sigma Theta voted in 1962 to discontinue the sorority's affiliation with ACHR. While the purposes and aims of ACHR were considered valid, it was felt that the structure was inadequate for their implementation. As a result, Delta has begun to develop her own program of social action and education through the Public Affairs Subcommittee of the Publications and Public Relations Committee.

Delta Sigma Theta's history is one of continual self-evaluation and readjustment to meet the needs of her expanding vision and program. In the sorority's voluntary departure from the "Greek-letter-type" image was the natural corollary of an ultimate withdrawal from organizations retaining it. Although still maintaining a token affiliation with NPHC, Delta Sigma Theta has made a sharp, irrevocable departure from the "Greek" world; but it must be remembered that her initial involvements with such organizations were the stepping stones which led to her wider and more meaningful affiliations.

DELTA CO-OPERATES WITH ORGANIZATIONS DESIGNED TO AID THE NEGRO

Delta Sigma Theta Sorority was born into an era of social upheaval and change, an era in which women were seeking equal rights as citizens and when Negroes also had begun the intense struggle for first-class citizenship. The NAACP was created three years before Delta's founding, and soon was followed by another organization, the National Urban League. Both were designed to aid the Negro in securing his rightful demands. As the sorority established herself beyond the need for concern about survival and status, she began to seek ways by which she could benefit the larger society. Delta's willingness to affiliate with other Negro fraternal organizations for the solution of common problems was a step away from a willingness to co-operate with all groups whose purpose was to aid the Negro race.

There is no record of the exact date on which the sorority began to lend its support to the NAACP, but it is possible that even in the earliest days some sporadic efforts were made—for an early *Journal* mentions "our alignment with the NAACP." But Delta could not long remain sporadic in her contribution to this organization pledged to work for the abolition of all forced segregation, lynching, and lawlessness, and to seek public education for Negro children equal to that of whites, the complete enfranchisement of the Negro, and the enforcement of the Fourteenth and Fifteenth Amendments to the Constitution of the United States. For many years the sorority has been a life member of the organization, usually making additional annual contributions of money through the local chapters, many of which also hold life memberships. For special NAACP drives, such as the Fund for Freedom, Delta makes additional contributions, both from chapter and national levels. Moreover, the sorority is represented at NAACP Leadership Conferences, Youth Conferences, and so on.

Delta Sigma Theta lends similar support to the National Urban League, whose program is designed to meet the needs of migrant Negroes in big cities, to ease the difficulties of mutual adjustments between employer and Negro employee, to acquaint the Negro with job opportunities in his community, to aid in the placement of Negroes in jobs for which they are qualified, and to push for equality in hiring practices. The Urban League also works for the improvement of working conditions in industries in which Negroes are employed and for decent housing for Negroes in urban areas.

While Delta Sigma Theta supports the Urban League financially and morally, she also maintains a special connection with it. From the days when her Job Opportunities Project was in its infancy, Delta has sought the experienced aid of the Urban League in developing its program. Delta *Journal*s are full of records of chapter undertakings in the field of Job Opportunities made under the guidance and with the co-operation of the local Urban League. In 1948, the two organizations undertook a joint venture and published a thirty-page booklet entitled *Negro Heroes*. The booklet, a color-pictorial, depicted the lives of famous Negroes, and was designed to serve as inspiration and a source of pride for young Negro America. *Negro Heroes* was also designed to supplement Negro history texts and to promote interracial understanding; it contains stories about such people as Booker T. Washington, Sadie Alexander, Toussaint L'Ouverture, Phyllis Wheatley, and Alexander Pushkin.

From their several joint concerns and their years of reciprocal support the Urban League and Delta Sigma Theta Sorority have developed a sincere regard for each other. In 1947, Lester Granger, Executive Secretary of the Urban League, wrote to the sorority, ". . . Between my organization and yours there must always be a strong bond of friendship and respect, for we especially depend upon college-trained Negro women for support and interpretation of the Urban League movement. As a national social agency promoting better employment opportunities for Negro youth and adults, better home conditions for Negro families, and a more effective leadership role for qualified Negro citizens the country over, the National Urban League needs and solicits the help of your great sorority."

Delta Sigma Theta also takes pride in its affiliation with the National Council of Negro Women, founded by one of Delta's beloved honorary members, Mary McLeod Bethune. A wide diversity of Negro women's groups are affiliates of NCNW. Besides college-based sororities, there are secret-order societies, missionary groups, and business, professional, and industrial societies. Altogether there are twenty-two national organization affiliates, whose members total 850,000.

The National Council of Negro Women lists as its purposes:

> To promote unity of action among women's national organizations and among all women in matters affecting the educational, cultural, economic, social and political life of America;
>
> To build a common fellowship of women devoted to the task of developing friendly relations among the peoples of the world;
>
> To collect, interpret, disseminate, and preserve information about and particularly affecting women;
>
> To encourage competent, intelligent participation by women in the spiritual, political, economic, social, civic, and cultural life of America, and to assist them in the development of these interests;
>
> To work for the complete elimination of any and all forms of

discrimination and segregation based on race, religion, color, national origin, or sex;

To establish an education fund to be used to promote educational projects, to give national and international scholarships and to publish articles, make motion pictures and employ other such media as is necessary to carry out such educational projects;

To make definite monetary contributions to recognized national charities.

Such large purposes demand large programs and large financial support. Delta is a consistent supporter of NCNW's program. Dorothy I. Height, Delta's past National President is now National President of NCNW, an additional reason for Delta pride.

Although when the need arises Delta lends her support to other organizations which contribute to the welfare of the Negro, her continuing activities are limited in favor of the organizations discussed. That the sorority does her best by these three is considered by the membership of greater importance than seeking other or more numerous avenues through which to accomplish the desired goals.

DELTA CO-OPERATES FOR THE TOTAL WELFARE

Delta Sigma Theta co-operates with numerous agencies and organizations whose purposes are humanitarian and without regard to race, color, or creed. This phase of Delta co-operativeness was a natural corollary to the development of Delta's program of service, and is therefore a relatively recent type of affiliation. World War Two had proved the futility of isolationist thinking, and the postwar years found Delta Sigma Theta moving swiftly into a larger understanding of brotherhood. While relinquishing neither self-concern nor concern for the race, she broadened her sympathies to include all those who were in some way needy of her services. In addition she began to work with several agencies through which she could best serve her own communities. When the sorority established the

Delta Five-Point Project in 1955-56, it was decided that rather than creating independent facilities to provide the services proposed, the sorority should seek to extend the services of existing agencies set up to do the job. Because the exact nature of Delta's affiliation with such organizations is explored at length in the next chapter, these are only listed and briefly discussed now.

One of Delta's Five-Point Projects is Delta Volunteers for Community Service, and it is in connection with this project that Delta affiliates with a larger number of agencies than in any other. The function of the project is implicit in its name. The sorority encourages member and chapter service to the several agencies in the community which are instruments of service to it. Certain criteria govern the selection of the agency:

1. That the organization be a national, private, voluntary social agency, designed to meet a social community welfare need such as housing, education, recreation, health or welfare service; that there be a degree of accountability to a community; that it draw broadly upon skills in social work, group work, case work, health education, and community organization;
2. That the organization makes efforts to have people of different racial and cultural backgrounds working together;
3. That there be opportunity for Deltas to learn new skills and concepts of community participation. This would imply that the agency take responsibility in training Delta volunteers;
4. That Deltas have the opportunity to be related to the ongoing activities of the agency, and
    a. that the agency accept qualified Deltas as active volunteers,
    b. that there be opportunities to be appointed to leadership positions within the agency,
    c. that there be opportunities to be elected to leadership.

On the basis of these criteria, Delta studied many possible organizations and decided to affiliate with the following: The Young Women's Christian Association of America, the American National

Red Cross, the Girl Scouts of America, the United Community Funds and Councils, and the National Urban League.

In connection with its International Project, Delta co-operates with CARE (Cooperative for American Remittance to Everywhere, Inc.), and with UNESCO (United Nations Educational, Scientific and Cultural Organization); through MEDICO (Medical International Cooperation Organization), now associated with CARE as MEDICARE, Delta was able to initiate the Mungai Maternity Wing in Kenya. On the undergraduate level, she lends support to the National Students Association of International Relations Clubs, and World University Service. In connection with her Mental Health Project, Delta co-operates with the National Association for Mental Health. Certain of these agencies are also utilized in connection with the remaining two projects, Library Service and Job Opportunities.

Besides her continuing affiliations, Delta is often invited to participate by sending representatives to conferences and workshops conducted by various organizations. In September of 1953, Delta Sigma Theta was represented at the United States Assembly of Youth, called by the Young Adult Council of the Social Welfare Assembly. This Assembly, held at Ann Arbor, Michigan, gathered together 300 young people between the ages of 18 and 30 to discuss "The World We Want." These young people of varied backgrounds and interests came together, not to make decisions for action in the realm of social and political affairs, but to pool and clarify their thinking about human rights and the status of the United States in the modern world. The Assembly offered a new avenue toward intercultural understanding, and Delta welcomed the chance of being represented by her Executive Director, Patricia Roberts Harris, and two other delegates.

The sorority is often represented at White House Conferences held by such organizations as the National Committee Against Discrimination in Housing. Sending delegates to such conferences is as much for the purpose of keeping the sorority informed on trends of thought and important legislation-in-the-making as for the purpose of lending support.

INDICATIONS

In her first half-century, Delta Sigma Theta has developed a wide diversity of affiliate interests. While she has strengthened her relationships with other Negro sororities, her bonds with Negro fraternities have weakened, albeit amicably and possibly as a natural development arising from the disparity in male and female interests. The indications are that in the future most contacts with Negro fraternities will be severed, except those in the nature of mutual courtesies.

Until the time when America has realized her ideal of democracy for all, Delta must continue and increase her support of those organizations which work to protect the underprivileged minorities. In most such organizations there is already interracial membership, and the future augurs well for affiliations with other interracial organizations. Delta welcomes every opportunity to share her thinking and experiences with other racial groups and to accept the benefits of association with white and interracial sororities, for it is believed that through fellowship comes understanding, and through understanding the true democracy.

8 *By yielding its fruits*

Delta's five public service projects

In 1955, a National Projects Committee was authorized to make an exhaustive study of Delta Sigma Theta's existing program of activities in order to determine its effectiveness; and, on evaluating its findings, to make recommendations to Grand Chapter as to the type of program the sorority should pursue in keeping with her aims, purposes, and resources.

At the first meeting of the National Projects Committee, in December of 1955, sixty-six responses to a questionnaire circulated to a sample of officers and sorors were studied in view of the committee's purpose. The questionnaire sought reactions to the effectiveness of existing projects and probed for further areas of civic and social concern worthy of project exploration. The findings resulted in the Delta Five-Point Project, which was accepted by Grand Chapter on presentation by the Committee.

The adoption of the Five-Point Project did not imply that each chapter was expected to pursue all five aspects of the program, for it was understood that chapter membership, resources, and interests, as well as community needs, would influence the extent of each chapter's participation. Indeed, chapters were emphatically warned against following the program in blind obedience. A guidebook was prepared, outlining the nature of each component project, the possible condition which would make its adoption feasible to a local chapter, and suggesting methods of implementation. Chapters were encouraged to share the findings of initial experiments with others and so make future undertakings easier for all. With this wide freedom in self-determination the program was begun, and within a year almost every chapter had made some effort, in varying degree, to implement the Five-Point Project.

The Five-Point Project is so called because it was felt at the outset that all aspects of the program were interrelated as they centered on health, welfare, and educational fields consistent with the sorority objectives, member interests, and community needs, although the purpose of each project is different. Thus the five "points"—*Library Service, Job Opportunities, Delta Volunteers for Community Service,* the *International Project,* and *Mental Health*—are collectively the Project. Although at first glance the International Project may seem scarcely related to the others, it must be remembered that the sorority has developed the bold vision of a world community, that it has established chapters abroad, and that it has always pledged itself to the assistance of the underprivileged and the needy wherever they are to be found.

The development of the Five-Point Project was remarkable in the history of Delta program for its planned and scientific approach. Hitherto Delta program, like Topsy in *Uncle Tom's Cabin,* had "just growed," arising out of immediate and pressing needs and developing by trial and error. The National Projects Committee was authorized when it became obvious that unless Delta made plans to concentrate her efforts in those areas where her contributions would be most meaningful, she would risk a feverish and fruitless scattering of her energies.

The Committee which developed the Five-Point Project was

composed of some of Delta's most qualified and knowledgeable women. Chaired by Dr. Jeanne L. Noble, now associate professor at New York University's Center for Human Relations Studies, and the twelfth National President of Delta Sigma Theta, the National Projects Committee also included Marietta Cephas, Gladys De-Priest, Vera Foster, Kara Jackson, Lucia James, Marjorie King, Bernadette Plummer, Thelma Radden, Maude Watkins, and an undergraduate, Mary Rucker. All except the undergraduate were professional women with a wide variety of the type of experiences to enable them to understand their work. They began their work on the theory that "We live in a day when what we decide to do must have a scientific base, reflecting our objectives as a national organization of college women." During the year of planning many consultations were held with outstanding leaders in the several specific fields. These leaders gave wholeheartedly of their time, interest, and professional knowledges and skills. In every instance there was a mutuality of concern and a sincere appreciation for what Delta was doing.

Among those with whom Delta consulted in developing the Five-Point Project were: Dr. Arthur J. Jersild, Teachers College, Columbia University; Dr. Allison Davis, University of Chicago; Dr. George Stevenson, National Mental Health Association; Miss Marian Densbach, National Mental Health Association; Dr. Kenneth Helfant, Rye (New York) Schools; Dr. Janet Rioch, Psychiatrist; Mrs. Catherine Lewis, Girl Scouts of America; Miss Virginia B. Smith, American National Red Cross; Mr. Nelson Jackson, National Urban League; Miss Ethlyn Christensen, Y.W.C.A. of America, and Miss Hollis Vick of United Community Funds and Councils, Inc.

On both chapter and national level, projects are undertaken after careful consideration of Delta's personal resources, including abilities, experiences, and training, and in keeping with the staff and financial resources of the organization. At present each aspect of the Five-Point Project is in a different stage of development. Perhaps the most often developed by the chapters are those two which were already in existence when the program was developed —*Library Service* and *Job Opportunities*—with *Volunteers for Community Service* running a close third.

Chapters are kept informed as to each other's activities by the Bulletin Edition of the *Journal.* At National Conventions conferences are held to determine the results of activities in each project and to guide the sorority as it makes plans for the next biennial meeting.

LIBRARY SERVICE

At the time when Delta Sigma Theta was planning its program of public service, the previously discussed demonstration library projects in North Carolina, South Carolina, and western Georgia were nearing completion, and no further demonstration projects were envisioned. But local chapters had expressed a continuing interest in this program, and it was agreed that Library Service should be maintained as a National project to be implemented on local chapter level.

In recent years there have been some interesting developments in this area. Often on their own initiative, chapters have broadened the scope of the project to include communication skills other than reading, and there has been some discussion about re-naming it *Communications Project.*

There are certain outstanding examples of the various ways in which the sorority has developed the Library Project. One such was the Southern Regional Hearing Project developed in 1957. National Hearing Week falls in May, and the Southern Regional Director, Thelma M. Cobb, saw this as an excellent opportunity to lay the foundation for a region-wide development of the Library Service Project. In making her report in the *Journal* on the Hearing Project, the Regional Director wrote:

> The very nature of the South, its complexity and dichotomy, provides a plethora of opportunities for the development of needed

> projects. This very ambivalence has served to limit, to a certain extent, the scope of any project which is introduced; yet Delta women have boldly accepted this as a challenge. . . . The Regional Projects represent collective efforts to meet the challenge.

The Southern Regional Project was initiated to point up the need for improved services for children with impaired hearing. Through the four areas of its hearing-conservation program—exploration, education, testing, and therapy—Deltas of the Southern Region were successful in developing "hearing consciousness" in areas throughout the South, where too little was known and far too little done in the way of providing services for children with hearing difficulties.

The focal point of the project was the establishment and operation of a Pilot Center to assist other chapters in the implementation of the project at the local level. The center, directed by Cecil Edwards, was located in Atlanta, Georgia, and was staffed with members from the Atlanta Alumnae Chapter, with the voluntary assistance of specialists and therapists in the areas of hearing and related fields. In addition to the services rendered at the clinic, the Pilot Center participated in the Annual Health Fair by administering hearing tests; an average of more than a thousand tests were administered annually. The Center also prepared and distributed brochures, pamphlets, and films that gave "helpful hints" for chapters and developed hearing consciousness for the several communities. Consultants were available on demand. The demand for more information which could be shared with groups interested in the project, led to the production of a 16-millimeter color movie, which told the story of the project.

Although the Pilot Center was the focal point of the project, chapter participation insured its effectiveness. Services in relation to hearing conservation were rendered throughout the region; members of the sorority served as speakers or consultants for Parent-Teacher Associations and other interested organizations; chapters assisted in the observance of National Hearing Week by displaying posters and circulating other materials published by the American Hearing Society, and by sponsoring chapter programs, several of which were broadcast over local radio stations. Wherever facilities or personnel were available, corrective therapy and follow-up treatments were provided for the subjects screened by the local chapter, and in other instances, chapters provided for corrective services through contributions to established community agencies.

Although this project is discussed under the category of Library Services, because aiding the aurally handicapped simultaneously improves their learning capacities and their communication skills, it relates to other areas of the Five-Point Project. The fact that several Deltas, inspired by the program, have chosen careers in the fields of speech and hearing therapy, relates to the job opportunities facet of the program. Certainly, as in its co-operation with the American Hearing Society, this project has some relation to the Delta Volunteers for Community Service. And finally there is the aspect of Mental Health. The child who cannot hear is often a disturbed child. When Delta brought sound to the ears of over two hundred aurally-handicapped children, a great step was made toward helping them to reach a degree of adjustment and in helping them to realize personal fulfillment.

The successful and rewarding Hearing Conservation Project was proof of Grand Chapter's wisdom in granting freedom of interpretation and implementation in developing the Five-Point Project, for it pointed up the degree of imagination and initiative Deltas can bring to Delta program. The Southern Regional Project proved how much the educated layman can do to meet the needs of the community and bring it to a new awareness of existing problems and ways in which they can be solved. In particular, the Project made the entire sorority aware that the Library Project need not be confined to the provision of books as a means of promoting public education. All forms of communication are the tools of education; therefore any program which is designed to facilitate communication is itself a tool of education.

The Project was ambitious and had certain inherent limitations, such as its technical nature and limited budget. An evaluation of the Hearing Project pointed up the fact that the exploratory and educational facets were the most effective, as shown in the inclusion of hearing tests in school health examinations in Southern areas where before they had been omitted, the increased awareness of the importance of hearing conservation, and the changing attitudes toward the stigma of impaired hearing.

As the Regional Director pointed out, the need for services to aid in the development of communication skills is greatest in the South where Negro children have so long suffered under an educational system separate and inferior to that accorded their white contemporaries. It is for this reason perhaps that the Southern Region has been in the lead in developing the Library Project.

Another outstanding development of the project also originated in the South. "Ride the Winged Horse" was a cultural development program for children which took place during the summer of 1957 at Tuskegee Institute in Alabama, a small but progressive community of about six thousand people. The core of the project was a developmental reading program designed especially to stimulate good reading habits in children in the sixth, seventh, and eighth grades. The Tuskegee Alumnae Chapter conducted the project with Hollis Burke Frissell Library of Tuskegee Institute as co-sponsor.

The project's title was derived from the Greek myth of Pegasus, the winged horse who carried the Muses through the heavens. Indeed, in the form of a small and winged, wooden horse pin, Pegasus became the emblem of transport to a delightful adventure for the more than fifty youngsters who participated in the project.

Pegasus arrived in Tuskegee because of a Delta's concern about stimulating her own children to a greater interest in voluntary reading of a better nature. The problem was immediate and not limited to her own family, for there were serious gaps in the cultural backgrounds of many people in the area. She took her problem to the Tuskegee Alumnae Chapter of Delta Sigma Theta, and the chapter welcomed the idea that it could do something to improve the child's motivation to better reading, granted the request for $25, and named a chairman and a small committee of parents, teachers, and librarians to explore and conduct an appropriate project.

Ideas, enthusiasm, and twenty-five dollars could best be utilized by expanding and enriching the children's library program already in operation. Before school was out, principals, teachers, and Parent-Teacher Associations at four local schools had endorsed general plans for the project, and formal announcement of Ride the Winged Horse was made during May Week when Tuskegee Alumnae Chapter presented an encyclopedia set to Tuskegee Institute High School.

On June 12, 1957 sixth, seventh, and eighth graders came to register for library privileges and membership in the special reading club. The children were expected to attend meetings on Saturday mornings during the summer. With the understanding that membership entailed reading books of their own choice, the children were given recommended book lists and individual reading-design aims, to help with balancing reading. Individual guidance with book selection was regularly provided. Those parents who accompanied their children had access to special lists and shelves arranged with materials on children's reading; such materials explained how the parent could best help the child develop better reading interests. Each Saturday, the Winged Horse emblem was given to children who had completed a phase of the reading program or who had participated in some activity.

The Tuskegee Project got underway with a variety of activities to stimulate the children's interest. The fifty-member group played literary games, such as identifying picture cards representing best-loved characters in children's literature. They watched films on *How to Read a Book* and *Improving Your Reading,* and both the mature and the younger readers were able to identify their good and bad reading habits as a result. As the season progressed, the interest increased and children often brought guests to share the Saturday morning treats. Members proudly and constantly wore their emblems to show they "belonged." The weekly newspaper carried feature stories about the project, and more and more children asked for admittance. One fond father called the project chairman to ask if it was too late for his boy to join "that horse club."

The project far exceeded initial expectations. The enthusiastic response of the children at each meeting registered their satisfaction. There was evidence that the children generally had shown increased interest, balance, maturity of reaction, and appreciation in the reading of books. The various activities had helped each child to progress toward greater sensitivities in experiencing books intellectually, emotionally and spiritually. A few children gave evidence of creative talent; many enjoyed new cultural experiences. For all, there was the reward of friendly association with and stimulation by youngsters from schools other than their own, and in a different kind of relationship.

There were benefits too for those who gave their time, energies, and talents to the project. Besides the satisfaction of a job well done, most of the volunteers maintained that they received more than they had given, in a better understanding of children and their needs. Several discovered new outlets for self-expression. Local teachers gained ideas that they planned to put into practice, for they were certain that the enriched experiences of the children who had participated would stimulate their classmates.

Delta is particularly proud of the Tuskegee Alumnae Chapter and its activity in this project. She is proud because the chapter proved what could be done with an idea, enthusiasm and twenty-five dollars—overspent by thirty cents—which went largely for membership pins and certificates, mimeographing, and postage. She is proud that the chapter understood that no real community activity functions independently of qualified community volunteers and agencies. She is proud chiefly that through the Tuskegee Alumnae Chapter, Delta was pointing the way to aiding children in areas where many advantages are deprived them by the local government.

There was an unforeseen consequence of no little import. It happened that Ride the Winged Horse took place at a time when there was considerable tension and turmoil in the Tuskegee community, occasioned by political action. For many in the community, the children's interests and activities, which were widely publicized, became a counter-force to civic strife. Moreover, the activities provided for the children themselves a means for maintaining emotional stability in a troubled adult world. For its children's cultural development program, the Tuskegee Alumnae Chapter won the annual community-school improvement citation, awarded annually by the B.V.D. Company.

Ride the Winged Horse had proved such a success that it has been repeated annually, and its scope has widened. In order to share the program with interested children who are not members of the reading clubs, the "Sunday Winged Arts"—a series of music appreciation programs, art exhibits, and book reviews—has been introduced. To involve parents in the project, "Parents' Winged Horse" was designed to help mothers and fathers select books and plan satisfactory reading and cultural experiences for their children.

At its 1958 National Convention, the sorority adopted the project as a "new look" for the National Library Project. Since that time, the St. Petersburg (Florida) Alumnae Chapter has also sponsored Ride the Winged Horse in St. Petersburg and in Bradenton, Florida.

Most Delta chapters in some way pursue the Library Project. Over 90 per cent of the chapters contribute funds for library equipment, including magazine racks, bookcases, display fixtures, art work, library wagons, and reading ambulators. Many chapters give books to children in the community, sponsor story-hours, and contribute books to schools, hospitals, and libraries. One successful activity fires another, and often an unexpected outcome is that many inactive Deltas become interested anew when a chapter's activity is made known. In seeking to deal with certain unmet community needs—not as problems but as opportunities for sorority service, Delta Sigma Theta usually reaps her own large dividends.

JOB OPPORTUNITIES

The Job Opportunities Project was initiated in 1941, and since then it has been a popular and contributing part of Delta's National Program. Answers to the questionnaires sent out in 1955 by the Projects Committee proved that interest in this projects area was extremely high—and this was not surprising. For years, Negroes have tended to concentrate in less than a third of the occupations available in American society. Among the reasons for this are a lack of knowledge of or motivation for entering the non-traditional occupations. With the doors of segregation at last beginning to open under the constant hammering of right-thinking citizens, colleges and leaders now face the question of guiding Negroes students into occupations not traditionally secure for them, but nonetheless desirable for those with aptitude. Delta Sigma Theta strongly feels the need for concerted effort to aid modern youth in finding its right occupational place. A particular concern of the sorority is to promote the concept of work as a wholesome activity, basic to human happiness. Psychologists have pointed out that a lack of attention to this concept on the part of parents and teachers militates against the child's motivation. Therefore Delta seeks to provide motivation as well as job information, and is active in several aspects of Job Opportunities:

1. Dissemination of occupational information, including educational requirements necessary for jobs and available scholarships;
2. Helping youths identify and harness their potential for entering occupations;
3. Encouraging counselors, business personnel, and others to guide and place Negroes in jobs for which they are qualified;
4. Aiding parents in their understanding of job opportunities.

On the national and regional level Delta has held pilot Job Opportunities Career Conferences on various college campuses in co-operation with the National Urban League. Companies and organizations have sent representatives to stimulate Negro youth to enter varied occupations and have themselves been informed of the availability of talent among Negroes. Believing that it is better to do a good job in one place than a fair job in many places, the sorority, together with the Urban League, moves into a specific community and there sponsors an intensive Career Conference. Here, young people are given vocational guidance and are provided with solid grounding from which the local communities continue to work after the conference moves to another area. Follow-up contacts have shown that many youths have been helped in finding their right occupational places as a result of these conferences.

Following the successful series of pilot programs in job opportunities, chapters began to adapt the project to the needs of their individual communities, and as with every project, chapters vary in their approach to Job Opportunities in accordance with the needs of the community and chapter resources. Usually, chapters undertaking a pilot program enlist the aid of the Regional Director. Grand Chapter has suggested for local chapter use, certain areas of focus:

1. *Parents' Clinics*—Considering the scientific reports on the effects of parents' attitudes on the child's motivation, this is a fertile field. Chapters often set up series of meetings with parents of ninth-grade pupils.
2. *Ninth-Grade Clinics*—This tends to be the grade at which occupational choices crystallize. Job opportunity clinics on this level prove helpful to home-room teachers and to parents.
3. *Search for Future Scientists*—This is a research program requiring close work with testing experts. Certainly some of America's future scientists are Negroes, but those with potential must be discovered.
4. *Conferences for Counselors*—The challenge of integration is not yet fully realized. Lack of contact between the two races has led to many stereotyped concepts of Negroes on the part of whites, and vice versa. In integrated cities, Delta chapters undertaking this aspect of the project issue invitations to leaders and counselors of all races in order to foster new understandings. Wher-

ever such conferences are held it is understood that even counselors need guidance to cope better with the problems of those they guide.

Since 1935, numerous Job Opportunities Conferences have been held in many cities by many chapters of Delta Sigma Theta, and some have been outstanding in their success. After a pilot conference held in Indianapolis, Indiana, in March of 1959, Dr. Allison Davis, professor of Education and member of the Committee on Human Development at the University of Chicago, wrote to Delta's Executive Director: "Looking back at the Indianapolis Conference, I feel that Delta has struck 'pay-dirt' in the field of educational counseling in Negro-white situations. No other organization, I believe, is directing its efforts to this specific need, although the Anti-Defamation League is working on integration as a whole. Counseling and the clarification of the psychological factors involved in integration are the very center of the whole process, it now seems clear. Delta had great insight deciding to concentrate on this pivotal area. You have the most effective and enlightened organization I know—bar none."

While happily accepting the compliment, Delta is constantly seeking to enlarge and enrich her program of Job Opportunities, and at the same time to enlarge her understanding of the needs in this area. At a time when the social and economic system is being revolutionized all over the country as regards Negroes, the sorority looks with concern toward the young people who will face the period of adjustment to a new order. Aside from ascertaining the aptitudes of a student who may enter a profession hitherto forbidden to Negroes, concern must be given his psychological fitness: Will he be able to withstand the psychological pressures attendant upon his entering the new field? How can he best be helped to understand and accept his role of pioneer for those who will follow, if the particular occupation is one he truly desires? Problems such as these were discussed at a Ninth-Grade Guidance Clinic held at Grambling College, Louisiana, in January, 1960. This national conference—which included such eminent consultants as Dr. Paul I.

Clifford, Professor of Education, Atlanta University, Atlanta, Georgia; and Dr. Max Wise, Professor of Education, Teachers College, Columbia University, New York City—had as its theme: "Raising the Aspiration Level of Minority Children."

In Shreveport, Louisiana, in 1958, a conference was held for ninth-grade home-room teachers. At the time of the conference few trained counselors were available to Negroes in that city, and Delta sought to improve the situation by acquainting the home-room teachers with some possible methods of guidance. Many teachers reported that the conference had enabled them to act in an area where before they had only had desire to do so.

In setting up career and guidance conferences, the chapters enlist the aid of other agencies whenever possible. Schools and colleges are usually glad to co-operate, as are local Associations of Guidance Workers. It is such co-operation that in recent years has inspired and encouraged more and more chapters to attempt an implementation of the program. And it is due to the co-operation of eminent authorities in the field that chapters have begun to overcome their qualms about overstepping their bounds as laymen. It is interesting that, as an initial step, many chapters undertake grade-school conferences, usually on sixth-grade levels, to guide children into discovering aptitudes which may later be useful in choosing high-school subjects. Such chapters usually discover that it is as easy to conduct a ninth-grade conference, and they proceed to do so on the next occasion.

Again in this area, Delta has reaped some unexpected rewards. Among these is the fact that this program, perhaps more than any other, has helped to bring Delta graduates and undergraduates closer together. Here is one of the areas in which the undergraduate can maintain a high level of interest and activity. Youth is always interested in the problems and affairs of youth, and by being called upon to participate in such conferences, the undergraduate feels useful, needed, and related to her graduate sister.

DELTA VOLUNTEERS FOR COMMUNITY SERVICE

In 1955, when the Projects Committee decided that "Delta Volunteers for Community Service" should be one aspect of the Five-Point Project, the committee was not presenting a new idea. Numerous Deltas through the years had given their services voluntarily to the designated agencies—the YWCA of America, the American Red Cross, the National Urban League, the Girl Scouts of America, and the National Community Chest and Councils—but the Committee felt that such participation was not widespread enough among Delta membership. These agencies depend upon volunteers in order to be able to make their greater contribution to the community's health, welfare, and recreational needs. Without volunteers, they would eventually cease to exist. The Committee therefore proposed that, through this project, Delta Sigma Theta lend its active and united support to these five agencies whose objectives are consonant with Delta ideals.

There was a subtler element of consideration in making this decision, for the sorority realized that in making available its manpower to these agencies, she would be serving not only the agencies, but also the needs of the individual volunteer. Volunteering to make a worth-while contribution to others is an expression of self-respect and a belief in one's personal capacities and abilities required for the job. In accepting the responsibility for helping others, one affirms a personal dignity and declares a potential value to society. The Negro, although in every respect qualified to make such a contribution, often fails to volunteer for fear of being rejected or humiliated by racially prejudiced elements in the agency he wishes to serve. Such fears, although sometimes justified, are psychologically crippling to the potential volunteer. Every human being needs to feel an interrelationship with the society in which he exists and that as his society contributes to his welfare, he contributes in some measure to the welfare of the society. Delta, therefore, in affiliating with these agencies, was aiding her membership in attaining a desirable self-esteem as well as supporting the program of agencies which benefit the community.

In view of all these factors, the National Projects Committee listed as the purposes of the Delta Volunteers for Community Service Projects:

1. To encourage Delta women to take a responsible part in community life;
2. To project the resources of Delta, namely her potential membership of 30,000 capable college women, into the community and nation;
3. To participate with national social agencies whose objectives are consistent with Delta ideals;
4. To increase the members' social sensitivity so that they are able to comprehend and assess community problems and make effective contributions toward their alleviation;
5. To build a reservoir of skilled and enlightened women who contribute meaningfully to the ongoing program of community agencies.

In launching the project the sorority employed a slogan: Every Delta in the U.S.A. an active responsible volunteer.

In view of the accepted procedure for launching a new project, the Grand President, Executive Director, Eastern Regional Director, and Project Chairman met on March 29, 1956, to discuss the possibility of the initiation of the pilot project in the Eastern Region; on April 24th, a consultation meeting with representatives from each agency was held in the Conference Room of the National Social Welfare Assembly in New York City. At that meeting a basis for co-operation between the sorority and the agencies was established and later was made official by each agency.

The next step involved planning the pilot area conferences. In order to orient a group of Delta core leaders, a planning session, again with representatives of each agency present, was held in New York on September 29-30th, 1956, at the Carnegie Endowment Center for International Peace. The first day was devoted to helping the Delta representatives gain a full understanding of the five agencies—their purposes and programs, and the place of the volunteer. During the next two days the Deltas were given intensive briefing in role-playing, discussion methods, and other techniques for conducting the area conferences. These selected Delta women all were qualified and successful workers in various fields of social work and their background of understanding helped them to groom themselves further for more effective leadership in the conferences.

The Eastern Region Pilot Conferences which followed were held in Baltimore, Maryland, Rocky Mount, North Carolina, Boston, Massachusetts, Newark, New Jersey, Roanoke, Virginia, and Charlotte, North Carolina. At these conferences the resource people who had been trained for leadership in the Delta Volunteers for Community Service programs worked with the conference participants instructing them in such matters as the need for volunteers, the techniques and procedures of becoming a volunteer, the organization and structure of the agencies, the training necessary for a particular type of volunteer work, and the kinds of volunteer opportunities available. Also present at each conference were representatives from the local branches of the agencies, who assisted in showing how certain abilities and skills could best be translated into action on the local level.

With this kind of grass-roots training, Delta Sigma Theta is ready to put the project into action. Each chapter undertaking the project is supplied with outlines of procedure. The first step is always the initial workshop at which Deltas are instructed on "What Makes a Good Volunteer" and at which the local chapter and the local agencies work toward a smooth and organized interrelationship. Then the chapter appoints a Placement Chairman who is responsible for the program and who acts as liaison between the chapter and the agencies.

The Placement Chairman may select a small committee with which to work, and she is responsible for finding volunteer opportunities in the agencies. She does this by calling on the person at the agency who is responsible for volunteers and explaining the purpose and intent of Delta participation, and finally by discussing the placement of Delta in volunteer spots; she is also responsible for explaining the agencies to the chapter. Often, at the request of the Placement Chairman, agency representatives come to speak to the chapter or to participate in a question-and-answer period or a panel. The Placement Chairman also keeps the chapter informed about the progress of the project. She keeps a record of each volunteer's experience with an agency as supplied by it. This is a confidential report designed to give the volunteer a criterion for improving her volunteer service wherever necessary.

Although most chapters have participated actively in this project, it cannot be said yet that the sorority has reached its goal: Every Delta in the U.S.A. an active responsible volunteer. But it is true that the majority of those who have chosen to be active volunteers have been responsible ones. The five agencies chosen for the project have offered wholesome outlets for Delta potential, and much credit is due them for their impartial and cordial incorporation of Delta volunteers into their ranks. Sorors in many communities have been chosen to serve on Executive Boards of the agencies; many Deltas are serving as instructors; thousands are making the routine regular contributions which keep the agencies alive. About these volunteers, a distinguished white leader in one of the agencies exclaimed, "Where have all these bright women been all my life? They are an untapped resource!"

THE INTERNATIONAL PROJECT

In deciding on areas of focus for Delta program, the National Projects Committee weighed each possibility against three vital questions: Were the needs of a proposed project acute enough to justify its existence? Was Delta Sigma Theta adequately equipped in skills and resources to implement the project? Would the adoption of such a project provide an avenue for enriching the personal lives of Delta women?

In proposing the International Project as an aspect of Delta program, the Committee was activating a concept of the Delta woman which had begun to take root in the sorority through the efforts of many farsighted Delta leaders. The Delta woman is not only a college-bred member of a college-based sorority, and is not only a member of a minority race whose concern must include all members of her race, and is not only a citizen of a community, a state, and a nation; she is also a citizen of the world, and in a world comprised of billions, she has a role to play. This is no easy concept for Deltas in small communities, especially in those communities constantly besieged by racial problems, to accept. But the Committee believed that a project with international implications would enable Delta women to broaden their knowledge and understanding of nations other than their own, to increase their interest in international affairs, and to aid in their developing a greater appreciation for people of different backgrounds and cultures. It was further believed that in some small way Delta could be of some tangible assistance, however minutely, in the solutions of the world's problems. Amid the conflict of ideas and ideals promulgated throughout the world, intelligent understanding as well as active support of the democratic affairs of nations must endure.

Through the International Project, Delta aligns herself with other organizations striving to promote peace and world fellowship. The first activity in this area began with efforts to aid in a disaster situation in the Republic of Haiti in 1955, when millions of dollars' worth of damage was caused by Hurricane Hazel. Aside from her humane concern for the Haitian Republic, Delta had recently established a chapter there, and thus felt especially close to the problem.

The village of Jeremie was probably the hardest hit on the island. The citizens were eager to help themselves and willing to work, but they lacked tools. The people of the village desperately needed a road from the village to the market, some twenty miles away through the jungle. But the men of the village not only lacked the tools with which to cut through the jungle and lay a firm roadbed; they also lacked the strength with which to do it, for food was scarce and the men were weak from hunger.

When Delta Sigma Theta heard of the plight of this village, she decided, under the direction of National President Dorothy I. Height, that help must be sent to the villagers. CARE, through its experience in its "Freedom Village" programs, seemed to be the logical organization through which aid could be sent and supervised. The sorority joined with CARE in the project and made its first contribution of $1000 to buy road-building tools and other self-help aid for the desirable goal of making the village economically self-sufficient—the villagers could sell their produce if they could get to the market. The money was immediately translated into enough barrows, picks, shovels and machetes, purchased locally, to build the road. In addition, sewing machines were sent to enable the women to produce articles for marketing and clothing their own families; and food was sent to strengthen everyone.

As a result of the first $1000 sent by Delta, the economic level of the village was raised so much that CARE warned the sorority against making further contributions which could create an economic and social imbalance in the whole area. Moreover, government conditions in Haiti were unsettled at this time, and since the people of the village had now found a way to help themselves, the project was terminated; but Delta was glad to have supplied tools to encourage the people.

The International Project is the only one of the five which is most largely implemented on the national level. This is natural, because it is logical that large-scale problems should be met with the concerted action of the sorority. Delta Sigma Theta also pursues its International Project by apportioning some of its scholarship funds for students in foreign countries. The sorority grants two annual scholarships to students at the Delhi School of Social Work in Delhi, India. Many Deltas have visited this country and returned impressed with the problems and progress of the people, and in particular with the courageous persistence of Indian women in securing their equal rights.

Often, aid is granted in small but heart-warming ways. In 1956, a native of Ghana was studying dress design in the United States and wanted a sewing machine to take back to her country where she could put it to use. Delta came to her aid with a new Singer complete with special attachments to do such work as putting on braid and making special stitching. On her return to Ghana, she reported to the sorority that she was now the leader in developing the Western styles which many of the young women wanted, and that her bridal outfits were the prettiest in the country.

The maternity wing in the Chania Medical Center is being built and equipped by Delta Sigma Theta because of a large concern for the women of Kenya who suffered from lack of pre-natal, obstetrical, and post-natal care. The enthusiasm engendered in the sorority for this project led Delta to enlarge upon the initial objective —equipping the maternity wing when it was built—by also undertaking at the 1960 Convention to finance the completion of the wing itself.

In October of 1959, Delta Sigma Theta financed passage from England to this country for a young Tanganyikan woman. Tanganyika, formerly German East Africa and now a republic, was at the time an East African trust territory administered by Britain for the United Nations. Like many other African nations, Tanganyika in 1959 was moving toward self-government. Lucy Lameck, a young leader and a nurse who had taught herself to read and write before finally receiving a delayed formal education, wanted to come to America to observe and participate in women's organizations and unions in preparation for the task of helping her people achieve political independence and aiding their social and economic development. Studying under a scholarship awarded by the Tanganyika African National Union, Miss Lameck had just completed special courses at Ruskin College in Oxford, England, in preparation for her coming role.

An anthropologist who met Miss Lameck in Africa was impressed with her potential and recommended her American sponsorship to Delta Sigma Theta. The sorority willingly accepted the idea and planned an extensive tour of the United States for the Tanganyikan woman who would be a guest in each chapter city. In return for its sponsorship the sorority hoped to gain a deeper understanding of the problems Africa faces today. In view of her plan to organize women's groups in Tanganyika when her country should attain independence, Miss Lameck found it valuable to study various organizations in this country, observing how they chart their progress and how they learn from their experiences. But unfortunately her tour had to be cut short because of illness, and she returned to Africa having visited only ten of the twenty-two cities scheduled. Nonetheless, the sorority felt that many reciprocal benefits had accrued from her visit. Certainly the sorority had acted as a good-will ambassador for the United States in enabling this woman leader to take back to her country a favorable impression of conditions here.

The International Project is also implemented in some measure on the local chapter level. Many chapters grant scholarships to their own members who wish to study abroad, and through the reports of the returned students the chapters broaden their own horizons.

Directives from the Executive Board enable the local chapters to do something tangible in their communities to increase their understanding of other nations' problems as they relate to the United States. It is stressed that *understanding* is the key word in the purpose of the project. It is not enough merely to give money. Some suggestions from Headquarters include:

1. Choose *one* country. Write to its embassy in Washington for literature about it;
2. Know the CARE program. Secure information from CARE headquarters;
3. Know the UNESCO program. Secure information from UNESCO;
4. Invite students from other lands into your homes, and invite them to address your chapter meetings;
5. Have local experts on international affairs address sorority meetings or participate in other programs.

The Far Western Region was chosen to make the pilot experiments in local implementation of the International Project. Some of the developments here point again to Delta ingenuity. Deltas in the Bay Area decided to contribute to a revolving fund to be used as helpfully as possible for foreign students who may find themselves in financial difficulties so far away from home. The contribution was made to the International House at the University of California at Berkeley. Deltas in Seattle, Washington, presented Ghanaian students to the public, and these students talked of the customs and educational, cultural, and political life of Ghana.

Many Farwest Deltas made movies while abroad to share with their sorors on returning to this country. The Sacramento Chapter invited 32 foreign students to a tea. The Los Angeles Chapter sponsored a forum which had as its theme, "International Implications of the Emergence of African States." The discussion took place before a capacity audience between authorities on the subject, who were either native Africans or who had traveled extensively there. The San Francisco Chapter held a "Feast of Nations" at the Y.W.C.A. to which people of all nations were invited and where food from many nations was served.

It will be noted that much emphasis is placed on countries inhabited by dark races. It is understandable that Delta should choose to make her initial efforts in and toward countries whose distant origins she shares. It is expected that for some time there will be among Deltas a special interest in Africa, for in every area of that vast continent the rumblings of freedom awakening are being heard. As members of a minority whose own freedom is still being sought, Delta cannot help but take sympathetic interest in other races whose sole stigma, it seems, is the color of their skin. As the project is developed further it is hoped that the scope will widen, at least to some degree, to include those of other origins who may wish to share with Delta their friendship and interests.

There are, admittedly, certain weaknesses inherent in Delta's International Project. For example, in many instances the Southern Delta has little or no opportunity to communicate with students from other lands. Southern patterns of segregation prohibit communication with whites whatever their nationality, and visitors of darker races vehemently shun the South—except the few Africans who may make brief trips there out of curiosity and the few studying at Southern colleges. The Indians and Asians who find their way South, as a rule prudently forbear any contact with Negroes for fear of being identified with them. Therefore, such a program, except by financial contribution and abstract study, or vicariously by the visit to another country by a Southern Delta, is impractical in some of the sorority's regions.

Moreover, there is some question as to the importance of Delta's gestures in this direction. But while it is obvious that Delta's efforts to promote peace and good will can, in all honesty, have little effect upon nations and their interrelationships (and the sorority does not deceive itself that they do), it is felt that the efforts of the sorority do have an effect upon the individuals they touch—an effect whose total impact can never be totally estimated. Most importantly, the very effort leaves its desired mark on the participating Delta whose understanding of the wider world has been broadened and deepened.

MENTAL HEALTH

The decision by the National Projects Committee to make Mental Health an area for Delta focus was not a hasty one. Every aspect of adopting the project was carefully considered. Did Delta have the resources, human and financial, to develop project activity in this area? Would Delta membership respond favorably to such a project or consider it too ambitious for them as laymen? Certainly, there was no question as to the acuteness of the need for such a project, for mental illness is the nation's number one health problem: Over 10 million people in this country suffer from some form of mental illness; almost half of the hospital beds in the United States are occupied by mental patients; one in every twelve persons, it is estimated, will be hospitalized for a mental disorder in the course of his lifetime; and one in every ten youngsters alive today will need psychological care at some time during his life.

Negroes live under social conditions which pose additional

threats to mental health. Segregation has been known to affect adversely personality development. The Supreme Court Decision of 1954, that segregation in public schools is unlawful, included in its statement: ". . . [segregation] generates a feeling of inferiority as to their [Negro children's] status in the community that may affect their hearts and minds in a way unlikely ever to be undone. . . ." There are also social changes which militate against the Negro's mental health: an aging population which feels the terror of uselessness; a teen-age population which feels the stresses of an era of a painfully evolving desegregation; and a highly technical trend in national life which, without care, may further de-emphasize the worth of the individual.

From replies to the questionnaires distributed by the Projects Committee, it was learned that a preponderance of community problems are related to Mental Health: How one feels about himself and others, and how to live with self and others. The manifestations of community problems can be juvenile delinquency or racial prejudice, among others—but the causes are psychological.

The sorority favored a Mental Health project, and, heartened by the interest of the sorority body as a whole, the Committee began to lay the ground work for it. Because of its scope, it was the last of the five projects to be tackled. In the interim there was a heartening development: The Central Region took the initiative and held a Mental Health workshop in Topeka, Kansas, in November, 1956. Sorors from chapters in the region gathered to hear such experts as Karl Menninger and such state consultants as Lelia Myers point up the need for organizations like Delta to give aid in this area. The Delta group was also given a blueprint for working with state agencies charged with the responsibility of Mental Health education.

The success of the workshop reinforced the committee's idea to propose a Mental Health Project to the sorority; and a careful study of the literature of agencies designed to deal with the problem and consultations with their officials were begun. Finally, a team of consultants was gathered together for a Mental Health Consultation with Delta officials. The Consultation was held in New York City at the Biltmore Hotel in June of 1956. The group of distinguished professionals included: Dr. George Stevenson, Psychiatrist and National and International Consultant for The National Association for Mental Health. Inc.; Dr. Arthur T. Jersild, Psychologist and Professor of Education at Teachers College, Columbia University; Dr. Janet Rioch, Psychiatrist, New York City; Dr. Allison Davis, Social Psychologist and professor at the University of Chicago; Dr. Kenneth Helphant, School Psychologist in the Rye (New York) Public Schools; Miss Marian Senbach, Field Representative of the National Association for Mental Health, Inc. Representing the Deltas were Dorothy Height, Nellie Roulhac, Patricia Harris, Letitia Johnson, Alma Marsh, Vera Foster, Kara Jackson, and Jeanne Noble.

The purpose of the Consultation was to discover areas of Mental Health activity in need of help from volunteer laymen, and in which Delta could assist with her human and financial resources. Out of this meeting the Projects Committee was able to develop a blueprint for implementation.

During the discussions, Dorothy I. Height, then National President of the sorority, voiced the hesitancy of the sorority to approach such a technical program. Dr. Stevenson replied, "As the majority of the members are teachers and social workers, Delta is directly related and has a great responsibilty in this area. . . . I have the feeling that the five-point purpose that you have spelled out in your preliminary guide provides the best springboard for things to be done. . . . We've read what you've been doing in Job Opportunity. Actually, you are already using a Mental Health approach, because when you go out to work with a full realization that it's important to help people have a healthy concept of themselves, you are using the best there is in the field of mental health. . . . Delta women are not laymen. You're professional people. We see you as colleagues, because you are teachers, you are social workers—persons with backgrounds of professional concern. . . ."

Dr. Rioch supported this argument by observing that, "The

teacher is a professional in the mental health field because her main business is child development. Society is moving towards a new pattern of living of which Delta women, mostly teachers, are a part."

Certain other statements made by the professional consultants concerning the need for mental health activity bear mentioning:

JERSILD: "Of basic importance is emphasizing what we have in common with all humanity rather than intensifying the differences. Negroes who are most accepting of themselves are more accepting of others; these do not identify themselves as Negroes but as human beings."

RIOCH: "One wonders if there is a need for joint planning for mental health of the white community because this is basically where the illness lies."

DAVIS: "The Negro woman in the South can do things men cannot do in opposing segregation, even though their careers are vulnerable. Delta is in a unique position is this respect, because it is a woman's organization and many of your chapters are in the South."

DAVIS: "Migration from rural areas is one of the causes of crucial mental illness. Schools and integration is another. . . . Integration is a great threat to many children because they have been insulated and if they stay within their own bounds they are safe; when they move outside they are hurt. . . . Negro students must learn that in order to be accepted they must work harder, compete more strenuously; or withdraw to original status in segregated living. Whenever a strong competitive group exists, where anxiety is involved, it is easier to withdraw."

On specific actions that could be taken, the leaders had this to say:

STEVENSON: "I think the community needs to be taught by concrete experiences that there is strength within the Negro population that can be of value to all. I do not think they will get this merely by words, but by seeing leadership in action."

JERSILD: "In order to help children with their problems,

teachers must begin to face their own. Mental health is a different operation from many other things. It is a slow process with little immediate apparent relationship to the ultimate. . . . If we are going to help our kids we have first to help ourselves. . . . What are some of the health-giving influences? Drawing on our own potential; improving our own outlook; helping others to realize theirs; group discussion; building security; building self-respect. Next steps involve a careful examination on the part of the responsible people in Delta with a long-term program of growth rather than a plan of immediate action."

DAVIS: "There are two possible ways of getting to the grass roots: family and school.

HELFANT: The most effective way for Delta members to move is through education. Why? Because most of the members are basically teachers."

STEVENSON: "Parent-Teacher Associations may be a good medium . . . and the member of Delta a good instrument for leadership with a P.T.A. Some ways of effecting action are: Work with teacher-in-service training; out-of-school training."

RIOCH: "Workshops in learning to talk with people are vitally necessary."

HELFANT: "Focus teacher workshops on 'What in us encourages or interferes with pupil growth?' This can be organized on a positive basis, but is generally ignored in teachers' colleges."

STEVENSON: "Specifically I should like to see the members of Delta put their hands to mental health activity in their communities and become more closely identified with mental health associations so that the interest that Delta has in mental health may be reconciled with and carried out jointly with mental health associations. And, of course, to that end we in the respective national headquarters would be glad to do some joint planning.

It was these suggestions and ideas that Delta used in the pilot project undertaken by the Central Region. As usual, the initial step was setting up workshops to provide adequate information, training, and professional guidance. The first mental health workshop, held in the Central Region, had been a success and paved the way for the second, which convened in Oklahoma City on November 3, 1956. Mrs. Leila N. Myers, director of the Division of Mental Hygiene of the State of Kansas, conducted the workshop. Consultants were Lester Hall, executive director of the Oklahoma State Board of Mental Health; Dr. E. P. Henry, medical supervisor of the Taft State Hospital; Mrs. Elnora Riley, recreational therapist; and Mrs. Corinne Lucas, director of special education for seriously retarded children. Gladys W. De Priest, who had been chairman of the Central Region mental health project, planned and presided over this meeting.

The Central Region adopted as its slogan, "Delta Spots Mental Health." As a result of the workshops, the chapters launched their individual programs. Money was raised to give such things as radios, television sets, toilet articles, games, and magazines to hospitalized mental patients. The Wekoka Alumnae Chapter in Oklahoma, in order to alert the citizens to mental health problems, sponsored a public forum whose theme was, "Improvement of Mental Health as an Approach to Peaceful Living." The St. Louis Alumnae Chapter held a public showing of a film entitled, *Back to Life,* and afterwards presented Miss Jeanne Adaniell, a psychiatric social worker at the Veteran's Administration, who gave suggestions as to what laymen could do to assist in fostering mental health in the community. (This effort won for the St. Louis Alumnae Chapter the 1960 National Projects Award.) Beta Phi, a mixed chapter in Denver, Colorado, held a one-day workshop under the direction of Dr. Franklin Wherry, director of the Mental Health Association.

On June 10, 1956, Gamma Beta of Topeka, Kansas, launched its program and assumed responsibility for finding boarding and adoptive homes for the "Forgotten Child"—youngsters whose minor handicaps hamper their adoption. Mrs. Dorothy W. Bradley, director of the Child Welfare Division of the Kansas State Department of Social Welfare, acted as consultant to the project. This chapter maintains a special interest in providing the basic needs of children—love, acceptance, security, protection, faith in self, guidance and control, moral and spiritual training—and sees its program as a means through which handicapped children may grow to be mentally healthy adults.

Through the initial efforts of the Central Region, Delta Sigma Theta was able to plan a nation-wide mental health program. Chapters have encouraged P.T.A. groups to show mental health films and to present consultants from mental health associations in order to alert parents and the general public to the dire need for mental health programs on local and national levels. Many chapters donate equipment to mental wards and mental hospitals. Workshops have been held in every region. This type of community co-operation has encouraged many citizens to new and active participation in mental health programs. Moreover, inter-chapter workshops on mental health have provided for Deltas themselves the opportunity to engage in extensive self-exploration and self-development projects.

Delta has been gratified by the response of schools and colleges to her efforts in the field of mental health. In 1959 Delta Sigma Theta became the first sorority to sponsor a course for academic credit. This was the Mental Health Workshop at Lincoln University in Missouri. The University readily accepted the idea of granting credits for such a course, and the first summer session proved so fruitful that the course now is a part of Lincoln's annual summer curriculum. That the course is well attended is of tangible weight in assessing a program whose benefits are largely intangible.

COMMENTARY

It has been observed that Delta adopted each of the five public service projects after much careful study, in each instance after applying the formula:

> Interest + need + resources, combined with study + consultation + experimentation = a Delta project.

The sorority believes that this formula will continue to assure good program, but recognizes that the possibilty of weakness in developing the program is not precluded. As Sara-Alyce Wright, a Delta leader who is a member of the National staff of the Y.W.C.A., points out in "What Makes Good Program?" in the May, 1958, *Journal:* "Too often program becames *a* tea, or *a* book review, or *a* special project, or *a whole bevy* of activities tumbling rapid-fire one after another. All of us, whether we come from fields of education, social work, the arts, or the sciences have said over and over again that all activity needs to be based upon a specific objective—which in turn is related to an over-all purpose and aim."

The Regional Directors and the National Officers try to be on the alert to see that the chapters understand fully the meaning and purpose of the Five-Point Project. Without such understanding, there is apt to develop an aimless and often feverishly fruitless round of activities. It has been heartening to note the constant improvements in the selections of activities by the chapters in implementing the program. Such constant progress is the result of the guidance of trained Delta leadership continually stressing the need for planning, involvement, responsible participation, and imagination on the part of the local chapters.

Early in the development of the projects it was realized that without sound leadership the whole program would soon collapse, thus the sorority did not trust to luck to provide the desired leadership. In 1956, the sorority conducted institutes for leadership training of Delta women in 27 cities. Twenty-seven chapters served as hostesses and many more attended, so that hundreds of sorors were participating in the series of Leadership Institutes held over a period of months. Such institutes are now a basic and integral part of Delta program; and out of them come those who ably interpret and direct the program of public service.

Delta feels that she is pursuing a good program. As a point of comparison with past programs, the Five-Point Project is typical of marked progress in Delta outlook and Delta approach. But it is not easy to predict future developments. It is certain that from time to time the program will have to be modified as new challenges arise and as the relative importance of needs shift. Even now, the sorority is occasionally challenged from the convention floor as to whether or not the present program is the most satisfactory. Are five areas of concentration too many—or too few—for the sorority's resources? At present the sorority is generally agreed that the current program is adequate to meet the Delta goals in view of Delta ideals; but frequent challenge and appraisal will ensure that Delta is always spurred to her highest and best. This is why when National Presidents address the National Conventions they invariably quote a line from *Alice in Wonderland,* which has in many ways become entrenched in Delta lore. To sorors who might think that enough has been done for a while along the lines of public service, the National President is apt to quote the Red Queen's advice to Alice: "You *see,* here it takes all the running you can do just to keep in the same place. If you want to go somewhere else you must run at least twice as fast as that."

9 *In multiple harvest*

Delta dividends

There is no period in the life of man or his society in which either may long and safely rest on his laurels. There is that impulse basic in life, which demands movement and change. While in nature such change is involuntary, man is able to influence the direction and the rate of the development of his mental, moral, physical, and spiritual faculties. But, even here, the refusal to respond to this instinct can respond in a withering of these faculties. Correspondingly, a society as an aggregate of humankind, may increase or decrease according to its nature and the wisdom of its leadership, but it may not remain static.

Delta Sigma Theta, therefore, does not regard the first half-century mark in her history as a summit of achievement. Such an attitude would result in a certain decline. But it has been said that organizations, like men, require fifty years to reach a full maturity; and as Delta Sigma Theta celebrates her first half-century anniversary she regards her present status as a plateau from which she may view her past record and evaluate the accumulated assets with which she may realize her future hopes.

At the 25th National Convention in 1958, the Executive Director, Patricia R. Harris, listed some of these assets and enjoined the sorority to accept the rewards of its efforts in the same spirit of gratitude as that held for the spirit of life and service. For the harvest of benefits which have accrued from fifty years of progessive service are not merely Delta's present pride; they are the seeds of her investments in the future. The Founders, who admit that the progress of the sorority has far surpassed all their early expectations, feel that in this spirit Delta is assured continued life.

DELTA'S HARVEST OF UNITY

In all the years of Delta Sigma Theta's development there has been concern for her unity. As the sorority grew in number and expanded geographically it was impossible to expect of the membership the sentimentality of sisterly devotion which had been the strength of the founding years, and the fact that such devotion would now characterize the local chapter constituted a threat to national unity. The emotional allegiance to the chapter and her members could possibly outweigh the loyalty of the individual Delta to the national body and could result in dissension and conflict. If the sorority was to grow in mutual harmony, the national body and its program had to appeal to sentiments and devotions larger than the personal ones which bind together the local chapter. In evolving a program of public service, Delta found that she was insuring her own unity while binding her membership together—not so much by the unrealistic appeal of a grand fellowship as through commitment to common goals in pursuit of which common personal needs could be gratified. During those periods in which fraternal organizations have been regarded with public disfavor, Delta Sigma Theta has sustained the allegiance of her membership because she has chosen to regard as synonymous her function and her program. She has promoted herself as an organization dedicated to public service rather than as an exclusive college-based aristocracy, and she has insured that her program is the result of a co-operative concern for the good of the whole through her democratic conventions, through a strong central government, and through the selection and training of wise and dedicated leadership. When at Conventions Deltas from every region link arms in the traditional fraternal gesture while they sing or say the words which speak of Delta fellowship, they affirm their unity, not necesarily in their personal relationships but in their devotion to Delta ideals. As long as the sorority is able to conceive ideals worthy of devotion and pursue them effectively, she will continue to reap her harvest of unity.

There is one aspect which has given the sorority much concern through the years—members who for one reason or another become inactive. It is to be expected that there will always be some sorors who are inactive; there are health and financial elements which can and do account for a member's failure to associate actively with her chapter. But there are also instances of inactivity which cannot be accounted for so easily. It has been noted that periodic lags in Delta's program correspond with a rise in inactivity. This is especially true of the graduate member who has other social outlets and to whom the sorority chiefly represents an avenue for service. It has been noted too that during the implementation of any project serving a valid community need the chapter is able to reclaim several inactive members.

Surveys have shown that the period in which the Delta member is most apt to become inactive is the one immediately following graduation. This is the period when the member has begun to take part in the responsibilities of the adult world; finding a job and adjusting to it, getting married, starting and maintaining a home take natural precedence over group associations, however worthy. After the member is established in the adult world, she usually seeks a graduate chapter with which to affiliate. There is, however, another factor which sometimes accounts for the interim of inactivity. The newly graduated Delta, released from the undergraduate chapter and from association with her peers often hestitates to align herself with the graduate group which is composed largely of older women. She is hesitant, not only because of an anticipated difference of interests, but also because when she was an undergraduate her opinion carried weight with her chapter—particularly in her senior year when she might well have held some office—and now she finds herself in a position of small importance and no authority in the graduate chapter.

Delta Sigma Theta has been aware of this problem for some time and has taken steps to solve it. The Yancey Commission was authorized in 1959 to explore the relationship between graduate and undergraduate chapters and make recommendations to Grand Chapter for improvement of the situation, some of which will be discussed in the final chapter of this book. But it was obvious, even before the Commission began its work, that something must be done to minimize periods of inactivity. Alumnae chapters require training in ways to attract and hold the newly graduated Delta, who should not only be welcomed but also be given equal status with other graduate members. In view of human nature and its regard for seniority, the sorority realizes that this is no easy task. But since hope for solution is implicit in awareness of the problem, Delta Sigma Theta believes that she is on the road to assuring the continuous activity of the individual Delta and so to improving the unified activity of the entire organization.

DELTA'S HARVEST OF WOMANPOWER

It was pointed out early in this history that her society has imposed upon the Negro woman a distinct and peculiar status. Generally, Negro women have been less subject to the racial discrimination and economic deprivation whose full brunt is borne by Negro men. Therefore, the Negro woman generally has been able to achieve more, educationally and economically. A study of Dr. Jeanne Noble, twelfth National President of Delta Sigma Theta, reveals that one in two married Negro women graduates have husbands whose occupations require less education than theirs; there are more Negro women than men who are college graduates, although the margin narrows yearly. Thus it is understandable that Negro women rather than men have assumed the greater number of positions of responsibility and leadership in their communities.

In recent years several thoughtful sociologists and historians have expressed concern about the behavior patterns of the Negro middle class. Important among these is Dr. E. Franklin Frazier whose books about Negroes in the United States include the much discussed *Black Bourgeoisie*. In a speech to the Delta Sigma Theta Convention in 1958, Dr. Frazier defined the Negro middle class in comparison with the class system which previously existed:

> Negro communities were once divided principally into two classes or . . . two castes. The upper class was constituted of those Negroes who maintained conventional sexual and family life. The father was generally responsible for the support of his family, and the children felt that they were the inheritors of certain traditions and that they were to pass on certain values to their children. This upper class resembled a caste in that family and social factors were more important than occupation, money, or success. A large proportion of these families were mulattoes or of mixed ancestry and although color was not the only factor in their social status it symbolized certain economic and social advantages. These families had inherited from white Americans, partly through the teachings of the white missionaries in the private schools, the genteel tradition or the tradition of the gentleman.
>
> *The new middle classes which have emerged have inherited to some extent this genteel tradition. But this new class is composed of other elements who exert a far greater influence on its behavior and outlook on life. I'm speaking particularly of the masses of Negroes with a folk background who represent an entirely different heritage. To be sure, there had always been a small stratum in the Negro community that was differentiated from the folk through education, new occupations, and land ownership. But one could not speak of a middle class of importance until recent years.*

> *There are two important facts to be noted about the Negro middle class. First, it has no history or tradition of commercial activities usually associated with the middle class in various parts of the world. Secondly, it is a class that depends upon salaries and wages. As the result of its social origins its traditions are those of the gentleman and the peasant intermingled in a way to produce much confusion in value and behavior* [emphasis added].

As a corollary to this definition, Dr. Frazier explored the theory that a lack of willingness on the part of Negroes to accept responsibility in the American community could be traced to the fact that as one who had never been taken seriously, the Negro had developed a playful tendency toward life, seeking to salve his frustrations in conspicuous consumption and superficial pleasures. But, as the walls of segregation are being broken down, the world begins to expect the Negro to behave as a mature person. Thus it is the responsibility of the middle class to lay the foundations for the more meaningful values and "to lead the way in becoming integrated as responsible persons in American life."

Since Negro women long have taken the lead in promoting higher intellectual and cultural values among Negroes in general, it is reasonable to assume that they will be found among those who seek to make their influence felt for the good of the whole. Surely, Delta Sigma Theta has been among the avant-garde in this respect. The days are long since past in which such considerations as social standing, physical beauty, and economic security can greatly influence admission into Delta's ranks. In fact, although such considerations have sometimes been the tacit policy of certain chapters, they have never at any time been endorsed or approved by the sorority as a whole. Delta Sigma Theta has always stressed the importance of wooing to her ranks those women with the potential and willingness for service who will enrich the sorority program and deepen her values. As has been observed, an organization which does not decline may be expected to increase. Therefore, Delta Sigma Theta does not take so much pride in the quantity of her numbers as in the quality of her membership. That these women largely are representative of the highest and best in womanhood is a tribute to the organization which attracts them. And it is in the quality of these women that Delta reaps her harvest of woman-power.

Census statistics as well as numerous studies show that the more educated the woman, the more likely she is to seek work outside the home. Since Delta Sigma Theta is a college-based organization, the large majority of her graduate members are employed, and usually in professional capacities. The sorority takes no stand on the subject of salaried occupation for women versus homemaking; but she is conscious of the fact that her employed members are in strategic positions in which can be obtained the training and experience these women can bring to bear in the sorority. This in no way detracts from the value to the sorority of the homemaker whose time and energies are less restricted than the worker's, and who may enjoy an even wider scope of intellectual and cultural pursuits. But it is interesting to note that for many years all elected Delta officials have been in positions of professional eminence.

Delta Sigma Theta does not minimize the importance of numbers because of her concern for the quality of her membership. To do so would be to defeat her own purposes for a large program demands a large membership. Nor does she delude herself that all her members utilize their separate capacities in pursuit of Delta goals. There are in Delta possibly as many "hangers-on" as in any other organization; but the larger the membership the greater the possibility of finding more potential leaders. And even the "hangers-on" serve to meet Delta goals in their financial contributions and moral support. It is Delta's endeavor, however, to sacrifice neither number nor quality, and this dual goal poses some problems of deep and continuous concern. In her speech to the 1958 National Convention, National President Jeanne Noble presented some aspects of this problem: "Requests have been made by chapters on large interracial campuses to lower the 80 per cent scholastic average Delta requires for initiation, to the average required by other

Greek-letter groups. Shall we become merely another social sorority or struggle to retain our uniqueness among Greek-letter societies on interracial campuses as a social group with emphasis on scholarship? Do we insist on maintaining our high standards, or do we compromise because other groups compromise? Shall we not work instead constructively together through National Pan-Hellenic Council, or Pan-Hellenic Inc., to raise the standards of Greek-letter organizations on our campuses?"

The sorority seeks and will probably have to continue to seek answers to these pressing questions. There is no gainsaying the fact that there is strength in numbers, but neither can it be denied that Delta's peculiar strength has been in the selection of the type of woman whose intellectual, moral, and cultural achievements have been the power of the organization. It is with these two facts in view that the sorority seeks, through her scholarship program, to improve the quality of the prospective initiate, and through leadership training to equip Deltas for their roles as public servants.

DELTA'S HARVEST OF LEADERSHIP

Delta Sigma Theta has shown wisdom over the years in electing to office those women most capable of filling the particular needs of the sorority at a given time. The qualities of leadership are easily recognized, and it is probably more noteworthy that the well-educated woman with a full-time schedule of personal activities who is elected by the sorority to National Office always has been ready and willing to fill it. Delta officials are not salaried and it is only in recent years that the sorority has covered their travel expenses. Moreover, being a National Officer in Delta Sigma Theta is no easy task. Besides accepting the burden of the responsibilities peculiar to her position, the Delta official may expect a full share of criticism —constructive and destructive—for there are always those who love argument for its own sake. The sorority is inclined to regard with indulgence these "irritants" who serve to keep the organization at peak performance in much the same way as the grain of sand is the stimulus to an oyster to produce a pearl. But it is the National Officer who is most often under direct attack; therefore her position requires of her diplomacy, good judgment, and humor.

In the preceding chapters several National Officers have been mentioned in association with particular events in Delta's history. It would be impossible to outline the achievements of all those who have held office in the sorority during these fifty years. Theirs has been service without glory, given for its own sake and because of their commitment to the Delta ideal.

It would be equally as impossible to list the achievement of all the women who have served as leaders in Delta chapters and as community leaders in keeping with Delta program. The thousands of women who have served in leadership capacities from the days of Delta's founding have left their monuments in Delta's continuous progress. Their service can best be understood in terms of the Delta concept of leadership.

In April of 1960, Vivian Washington, Delta's National Treasurer, defined the role of the Delta leader for the benefit of the membership. First she described the nature of leadership.

1. Leadership is a "helping" or "enabling" process in which the leader enables other individuals to fulfill their separate duties in attaining a common group goal.
2. Leadership is a relationship among people in which the leader seeks to understand the behavior and appreciate the worth of those individuals who are being led.
3. Leadership is a situational phenomenon in that a leader must be chosen to fill a specific situation. Good leadership in one capacity does not guarantee good leadership in another.
4. Leadership is co-ordination of effort. Leaders in a society must work harmoniously together for the good of the organization.
5. Leadership is a fulfillment of purpose, as it carries the major responsibility for helping group members understand and achieve their purposes.
6. Leadership is a process of meeting human needs. The leader must understand that in enabling the group members to achieve

common goals, she is also enabling them to experience personal satisfactions inherent to the motivation of the attempt.

Next were listed the attributes of the good leader:

1. A good leader assumes responsibility.
2. A good leader realizes the potential good of competition and uses it.
3. A good leader makes use of co-operation.
4. A good leader delegates authority.

The sorority is aware that it is not enough for the individual Delta to understand the nature of leadership and the role of the leader. At Leadership Institutes the techniques of leadership are fully explored; but also discussed are the subtler elements that must go into the making of good leader. In an article for the *Delta Journal,* National President Dorothy I. Height described the attitudes which much accompany the skills of leadership:

> . . . Leadership is not a function. It is one's response to the needs of the situation. Leadership is in every person throughout the membership. It is not a reward, but the opportunity to be the servant of all.
>
> Delta women are challenged to new dimensions of leadership. We must help one another sense and face changing cultural patterns affecting our role as women and as citizens. People the world over long to be accepted, not for what they look like, or what they have, but for themselves. World affairs are our affairs and the place where we give world leadership is right where we are on campus or in community. As we lift our sights, we develop ideas of how we may reach out to the world and make use of ideas that come to use from people around the world.
>
> Deltas know the need for knowledge and skill in all we do. The highest standards of scholarship and achievement are ours. But we know too that the greatest gift of the leader is neither facts nor tools—but her deepest self—freely shared. At this moment in history, the spirit in which every Delta woman gives of herself is more important than any set of rule or techniques. Let us make full use of all our talents and resources to strengthen the human relations so basic, to give quality to leadership in today's world.

In Dorothy Height's statement can be found the motivations which have produced the harvest of freely given service which is the foundation of Delta Sigma Theta. It is this free giving of self so frequently true of Delta leaders that has added the touch of genius to their leadership—the ability to extract the extraordinary from the commonplace, to help each Delta see in herself that special essence from which greatness is molded.

DELTA'S HARVEST OF GREATER MATURITY

A minority group can escape paternalism on the part of the larger group only in the measure to which it can prove its social maturity. In his speech to the 25th National Convention of Delta Sigma Theta, E. Franklin Frazier explained, ". . . that when a group subjects itself to self-analysis and self-criticism, it is a sign of maturity." The sorority has sought in increasing degree to estimate and analyze her structure, role, program, and usefulness, and her uneven progress in this area has often been tinged with conflict. Self-appraisal involves facing the possibility of the need to change, and it is human nature to be suspicious of change. Often when Delta's elected leaders have demanded a reappraisal of Delta values and Delta program, the initial reaction of the body was to reject the idea because in the status quo was a pleasant security. This was the first reaction when the Job Opportunities Project was presented for the consideration of the sorority; it was the reaction when the idea of a National Staff was introduced; it was the reaction to so simple a matter as the simplification of the existing system of nomenclature. That these changes all were implemented eventually, was due neither to a magical growth in amenability to the opinions of the leaders nor to the arbitrary imposition of will by the leaders upon the membership. The sorority has accepted ideas at first rejected because Delta officials have carefully accumulated all the relative facts and presented them to the body for consideration. It is fairly safe to say that on occasion the body has been shamed into taking the necessary action, when all the facts substantiated that a refusal to do so would be unworthy of the Delta ideal and Delta potential.

However, within the past two decades, there has been a marked improvement in the general willingness of the membership to take stock of the organization. The sorority as a whole has increased her concern for her role in an era of rapid and often startling changes. It would be difficult for an organization in this age not to realize that failure to keep step with the times could threaten its very existence. Delta's original purposes are unlikely ever to change; but in every period the interpretation of those purposes must expand to meet new challenges. It is this knowledge that has facilitated the series of internal studies and surveys made by Delta Sigma Theta in recent years, and out of the findings of these surveys and studies Delta has evolved her larger concepts and broader program.

Delta Sigma Theta is an organization dedicated, of her corporate volition, to public service. She recognizes the reciprocal relationships and rewards between those who are served and those who serve; therefore she does not seek to glorify her role. She makes no exaggerated claims to status nor to her importance in the scheme of things. On the other hand, her corporate existence precludes the need for affecting false modesty. The sorority constantly strives for a fuller internal recognition of her potential and realized values in order to assure the respect of the membership. Within the past decade Delta has developed a growing awareness of the need to tell the Delta story to the outside world, not to exploit her role for praise, but to make the public aware of the sorority and her program as an avenue through which the community may be served. The sorority can "go" to a limited public because it is limited in numbers; but with a knowledge of its existence, the public can "come" in larger numbers to the sorority. Hence in recent years Delta Sigma Theta has engaged a public relations firm to do this job.

One of the symbols of Delta's larger maturity is the establishment of chapters beyond the continental United States. The chapters in Haiti, Alaska, and Liberia represent a new era in Delta thinking.

It is obvious that the sorority has grown in its concept of "fraternity" since the days when bitter controversy was waged over whether or not students in Southern colleges should be admitted. But Delta is part of all the world that recognizes the castastrophe implicit in the conflict of ideologies at a period when man possesses the means to his own wholesale destruction. If the sorority is to act in consonance with her belief that it is of measurable importance to do what it can with what it has, it must be a leader in the area of "brotherhood"—in the sense that it must be willing to include as members those of every race and origin who are qualified.

Each of the chapters abroad was established by a nucleus of American-born Deltas living in the respective countries. But Delta has never intended that such chapters become the haven solely of the American Delta abroad. The founding chapters have been given specific instructions to seek to initiate more and more qualified women of the various countries, for it is to be hoped that the chapters abroad will take stable roots in the culture of the countries.

The problems in establishing chapters beyond the continental United States are many. The distances involved weaken communication with other chapters and the National Board: it is difficult, for instance, for the chapter in Liberia regularly to send delegates to Conventions. And there is the problem of programming for chapters whose needs are seldom synonymous with those of their sisters in this country. Because of this, many allowances and exceptions are made for the foreign chapters in the hope that as they grow they will make their unique contribution to the world in the name of Delta Sigma Theta.

Much has been said about the Delta ideal and its expression in the Delta program. And it could well be argued that, because what Delta does she does mostly in small and often simple ways in many scattered communities, the ideal is trifling and platitudinous. The sorority knows that the importance of her role and her program will continue to be questioned. But while she is personally convinced of the value of her program because of the fruits it has borne, she is more convinced of the value of her ideal. Delta agrees fully with those who point out that the ideal is far greater than the program, and she hopes it will continue to be so, for ideals so easy to attain are of small importance. It is in striving toward high goals that the sorority measures her own progress and assists her membership toward a greater self-realization and fulfillment. Dr. Ashley Montagu, anthropologist and author of *The Cultured Man,* affirms that man has deeper needs than the physical and the mental. There is also "the strange necessity of beauty, of love, the receptiveness to humane feeling, the sharing in and with one's fellow man, indeed in all things living and non-living." The Delta ideal is, most simply, the continuous fulfilling of these "strange necessities."

10 *The tree can endure*

Implications for the future

The 26th National Convention which convened at the Palmer House Hotel in Chicago, Illinois, August 12-21, 1960, had as its theme, "Appraising Values for a Creative Life in Freedom and Dignity." If this slogan bore none of the earmarks of the short, catchy phrase, it was the more indicative of the attitude and outlook with which Delta Sigma Theta, Inc., entered upon the deliberations that would usher in the three succeeding years which were officially proclaimed as the Golden Anniversary Celebration Period, to be climaxed at the 27th Convention in New York City.

Certainly the sorority was fully aware that the time was ripe for appraising values. Two years before, addressing the 24th Convention, Dr. E. Franklin Frazier had said, "Self-analysis and self-criticism are signs of maturity on the part of people, because they are an indication of a developed self-consciousness and the intellectual freedom which is a part of self-consciousness."

On the threshold of its second half-century, Delta Sigma Theta set for herself the task of appraising her status and her values toward the same end which in this era is the urgent demand of people, races, and nations the world over—the creative life in freedom and dignity. Never before in the history of the world has this basic hunger of the human heart voiced itself so clearly, emphatically, and universally as in this mid-century era. Nations around the globe struggle to free themselves from the tyrannies of those outside forces which would dictate their form of government and their way of life. Minority groups everywhere cry for justice and the establishment of human rights, and on the American scene, the Negro takes a giant step in finding ways to prod the national conscience towards recognizing the equal citizenship which is rightfully his.

In this last respect, there has been a significant revolution in tactics. Whereas previously the leadership for bringing to bear pressures that would promote the cause of the American Negro had lain largely in the hands of such organized groups as the NAACP and the National Urban League, there began in the 1950s an apparently spontaneous grass-roots upsurge in the struggle for equal freedom and human rights.

It is possible that these demonstrations were initially inspired by the precept and example of the Rev. Dr. Martin Luther King, Jr., who had been elected to lead the Montgomery Bus Boycott—a nonviolent demonstration in which for more than a year the Negroes of the city refused to ride the city buses until segregated seating was abolished—for all subsequent demonstrations have had in common an insistence on nonviolence and an implacable determination not to yield, evidenced by a firm disregard of the threat of consequences. Being fined, jailed, and abused have been accepted rather as badges of honor.

Across the nation, communities that have always kept the Negro segregated and isolated—barring him from public schools, parks, auditoriums, and libraries, from restaurants, swimming pools, and churches—have been shaken and often forced to yield by orderly, unified, and determined "walk-ins," "sit-ins," "wade-ins," "stand-ins," and "kneel-ins." To test the laws banning segregation of interstate travel facilities Negroes and many sympathetic whites have courageously embarked on "Freedom Rides."

What is most significant about this new trend is that it is mainly Negro youth who have taken the lead. Impatient with the slower processes of previous generations the Negro adolescents and young adults of today strain at the bit of second-class citizenship in a supposedly democratic society. They have the vision and intelligence to use the structure of this democracy to their advantage. If occasionally there is a lessening of deference toward prior generations on the part of youth today, it is the forgivable tangent of a long needed self-confidence and self assertion—of a people at last come full circle in self-realization.

These are the typical youngsters that comprise Delta's 89 undergraduate chapters. At a time when Delta's past is being evaluated to point the way to her future, it is natural and proper that a major concern be her undergraduates. To them will be handed the responsibility of steering the organization through at least the first half of the next fifty years. We can foresee that the demands and complexities of their times will increase. Will they be so equipped then with those values that will enable them, whatever changes are wrought in their world, to secure for themselves and therefore for others the creative life in freedom and dignity? Will this Delta tree, planted fifty years ago by youthful suffragettes and inherited now by young Freedom Riders, continue to thrive and flourish, serving itself and its community in the years to come?

In the full awareness that the organization was founded by youth and has been maintained through its history by youth grown to womanhood, Delta does not fear that this generation is less capable. She fears only failing to do her utmost in helping to develop these youngsters whose society will offer even greater opportunities for public service and make greater demands on individual potential.

For this reason, the theme of the 26th Convention was chosen in full realization of the task it presented for the Golden Anniversary Years. To this point, National President Dr. Jeanne Noble said in her biennial Convention Report:

> . . . As we gather today in this fading summer month, at the turn of a new decade, you and I are deeply aware that we are passing a boundary of history and the consequences of that passage will be felt in all aspects of humanity's life, dreams, and philosophy. No less will this impact of change be felt in Delta.
>
> Our awareness of the extent and rapidity of a changing world is only outdistanced by the growing, gnawing knowledge that something is amiss—things are adrift. Unsure of the world around us, facing strong social forces that threaten to dwarf and render us helpless as humans, we search for a firm footing. We long for a sure anchorage. Perhaps Captain Ahab of Moby Dick speaks for us: "I like to feel something in this slippery world that can hold."

To find and illumine at the close of its first half-century that which "can hold" is Delta's proclamation of her faith in her own continuity through the years.

THE YANCEY COMMISSION

During her lifetime, Dr. Sadie M. Yancey, longtime Dean of Women at Howard University in Washington, was vitally interested in helping the undergraduate. As Chairman of the Scholarship and Standards Committee of Delta Sigma Theta, she was a constant source of guidance and inspiration to the sorority in this area.

The 24th National Convention (1956) devoted a full day to undergraduate activity. A panel comprised of six eminent Delta women, all college deans, was led in discussion by Dr. Yancey on the topic, "Motivating the Undergraduate Potential." They were emphatic in their joint opinion that "Delta does not have an undergraduate problem, but rather a responsibility to its undergraduates."

It was under Dr. Yancey's direction that the Scholarship and Standards Committee recommended to the Executive Board that a special commission be appointed to explore undergraduate needs. Dr. Yancey died before Delta Sigma Theta had translated her deep concern for undergraduates into a formal commission to investigate this area. It was fitting that when it came into being in 1958, the Executive Board voted to name this group the Sadie M. Yancey Commission on Undergraduate Development.

A group of Deltas with particular research abilities drawn from the social sciences were appointed to be chaired by Sara-Alyce Wright. A dynamic Delta with wide experience in the social sciences, Mrs. Wright, as a staff member of the Leadership Services Unit of the National Board of the Y.W.C.A. bears special responsibility for the development of program in that organization for youth from twelve to eighteen years of age.

The stated purpose of the Commission is "to study and appraise the needs and potentials of undergraduate Deltas; and to recommend a national program that will contribute to the specific needs and interests of the undergraduate woman, a program that will enable her to make an effective contribution to her community, now and following graduation."

The Commission believed that its findings would serve as a guide to the undergraduate program and thus strengthen the experience of undergraduates to the end that their sorority participation would contribute to their growth as individuals, enable them to function effectively in the sorority as a whole, and inspire them to maintain their association with Delta following graduation so that the sorority's impact on community life would increase.

Gathered at its first meeting at National Headquarters, February 21-22, 1959, the Yancey Commission came to grips with its task. To be able to explore more fully the status of the Delta undergraduate, primary strengths and weaknesses inherent in belonging to a sorority required definition.

The Commission listed as strengths:

1. Opportunity for original and independent planning;
2. Sense of status;
3. Sense of identification;

4. Opportunity to know women of different ages and achievement levels;
5. Association in a formalized setting;
6. Experience in organization life;
7. Outlet (through ritual and amorphous idea of sisterhood) for adolescent idealism.

Among the listed weaknesses were several which are peculiar to a Negro sorority. Regarded as weaknesses were:

1. Lack of adequate supervision and guidance;
2. Ambivalent attitude of college administration toward the Negro Greek-letter society;
3. Time demands which lower scholarship;
4. Lack of appeal to the academically superior girl;
5. Segregated activity;
6. Lack of social sophistication;
7. Sense of exclusiveness;
8. Lack of program content;
9. Inability to relate classroom learning to extracurricular experience;
10. Expense of probation and membership;
11. Lack of satisfactory image comparable to that evoked by white sororities.

Armed with this knowledge and with their stated objectives, the members of the Yancey Commission then isolated the following areas as the major concerns with which they would be engaged:

1. It is important to recognize that as we work with undergraduate chapters we are working with persons in late adolescence, seeking for identification and a sense of self, still filled with the idealism characteristic to this stage of human growth.
2. We must constantly reappraise our goals and objectives as a sorority in light of the changing times and the changing needs and expectations of Negro girls in the college community today.
3. We need to know more about the undergraduates with whom we are working. Who are they—scholastically—in what fields

of interest—from what geographical locations—previous experience in group life—contributions to total college scene—marital status—travel and work experience—socio-economic background.

4. Recent correspondence and consultation with college student personnel staff and administrators indicates that priority considerations be given to improving and interpreting:

    Our pledge and probation system
    Our standard of the B average
    Our policy on sorority houses
    Our goals as an organization geared to help women participate effectively in community life, locally, nationally, and worldwide.

5. There needs to be more effective communication between the national office and college administration in relation to the above.
6. The pledge period must be more meaningful, providing opportunities for girls to experience in essence what belonging to Delta Sigma Theta really means.
7. A priority need is to work with advisors of undergraduate chapters to clarify their role, give status and recognition to them, and interpret some of the qualities and attitudes necessary for advisors to have.
8. We need to be aware of some of the reasons our number of initiations is not increasing. Is it poor scholarship? high cost of initiation? lack of appeal to scholars? availability of other kinds of college organizations which fill the need formerly met by sororities? others?
9. We must study current program and structure and provide materials and training opportunities to improve the undergraduate chapters.
10. We must study and try to enhance the relations between graduates and undergraduates.
11. There is a need for undergraduates to be related in meaningful ways to the total activities and experience of the sorority and

feel that they have a real part with graduates at all levels of operation.

By April of 1960, the Commission had compiled a comprehensive questionnaire to be distributed to every undergraduate Delta in 111 chapters. The 95-point questionnaire was divided into eight sections: Numerical, Marriage, Finance, Life Beyond Class Activities, Delta Activities, Social Values, Race Relations, Gains and Models. There were questions dealing with vital statistics; age, health, marital status, scholastic levels and ratings, religious affiliations, family relationships and status, personal tendencies, and attitudes and opinions regarding marriage and politics.

The section devoted to Finances was prepared in order to determine the economic levels and the pre-graduation employment of Delta students, and to determine also their attitudes about expenses incurred for membership in the sorority.

Questions relating to undergraduate Delta attitudes to and participation in extracurricular activities were designed to determine individual capacty for adjusting to and improving social communities. The section devoted to Delta Activities and Relationships sought to determine the status and function of each chapter as seen from the point of view of its individual members: its relationship to the college, to other Greek-letter organizations, to the alumnae chapter in the area, and finally to Grand Chapter.

Obviously, such an extensive study would require a long and intensive period of evaluation and the aid of experts. To assist in compiling and analyzing the findings, Delta Sigma Theta enlisted the aid of Dr. Robert Johnson, Research Director of the National Conference of Christians and Jews, and of three graduate students at New York University, all candidates for doctoral degrees: Mrs. Hilda O. Fortune, Director of Personnel Services for the National Urban League; Miss Harriett Blackburn, an honor graduate of Antioch College; and Miss Theressa Hoover, a member of the National Staff of the Methodist Board of Missions. With their aid, a book based on the completed analysis will be written and published. Currently, the Yancey Commission Study facts are being compiled and analyzed at the New York University Center for Human Relations. Although the study is not yet complete, certain facts have already been ascertained.

At the 1960 National Convention a day was designated as Yancey Commission Day. A group of panelists was invited to present to the sorority their views on undergraduate life. These were: Dr. Max Wise, Professor of Education at Teachers' College, Columbia University; Dr. Nevitt Sanford, Professor of Psychology at the University of California at Berkeley; Dean Margaret Habein of Wichita College, Wichita, Kansas; and Dr. Anna Harvin Grant, a member of the Yancey Commission and Professor of Sociology at Grambling College, Grambling, Louisiana.

Questions from an appointed Interrogating Panel of Undergraduates were posed to the panelists. From this stimulating session came an increased awareness that there is on the part of undergraduates themselves a deep concern for their present and future and a refreshing willingness to be constructively directed. Dr. Grant, assisted by Dr. Hilda Davis, a member of the Commission and Administrative Assistant to the State Psychiatrist of Delaware, made a statistical report on the findings of the Commission up to the 1960 Convention period. They presented the facts gleaned from the statistics that Delta undergraduates:

1. Do have B-average minds, but do not use them to the best advantage;
2. Come from stable homes, usually from working-class families;
3. Are for the most part being supported by their families, although an appreciable number earn their own fees;
4. Prefer to work after college;
5. Were influenced by families to secure college education;
6. Prefer a democratic home where decisions are shared;
7. Generally accept Delta's program as understood;
8. Confine their leadership abilities to sorority participation.

Some immediate areas for consideration were thus clarified. How could Delta be influential in motivating her members to fuller academic and social achievement? How could the Five-Point Project be further explored toward providing a creative and contributive channel for leadership and public service potentials? How could the sorority clearly establish for its undergraduates the public service image as being more than that of a purely social organization? How could a stronger youth-adult relationship be established?

The final analysis and recommendations from the Yancey Commission are expected to direct a stronger undergraduate program for Delta on both Negro and integrated campuses. As a long-range but vital objective, it is hoped by the sorority that in some measure the work of the Yancey Commission will identify and eliminate waste in Delta women's education—waste to society, and waste in terms of individual self-fulfillment.

THE CHAPTER AUDITS

While the Yancey Commission Study was devised to explore the status, outlook, and personal relationships of the individual undergraduate Delta, another tool has been fashioned in these Golden Anniversary Years in an effort to appraise the status, outlook, and relationships of both the undergraduate and alumnae local chapter. The Chapter Program Audit was initiated in 1958, taking the form of a series of questionnaires designed to gauge the atmosphere in which the group exists, intra- and extra-organizational communication, and the import of the "total Delta program," both traditional and public service.

There were four major areas of concern: Program Planning and the Use of Committees; Communications; Membership; and the Traditional Delta Program and the Public Service Projects. The Traditional Delta Program includes Founders' Day, May Week, the Jabberwock, and affiliate relationships.

So often have the facts derived from the assembled statistics of the four categories shown implications related to the other areas of concern, that no attempt will be made here either to separate the findings or to confine them to the area in which they were listed.

From the data thus far assembled and evaluated, many significant facts have been revealed—some heartening, some distressing. On the credit side is the statistical evidence that a healthy fellowship prevails within the local chapter; that it generally functions in an informal, co-operative and supportive atmosphere; that members are attracted to meetings by the Delta program, the fellowship the meetings afford, and out of their sense of devotion to the organization itself.

But there are indications to show that these meetings on chapter level are not sufficiently organized or efficiently executed to constitute a major appeal in themselves. The effective use of committees, as demonstrated by Grand Chapter, has yet to be fully mastered at the local level. This lack is not so innocuous as it would appear at first consideration. The primary medium of communication from Grand Chapter to local chapter is the periodic chapter mailing. These mailings are directed to the chapter presidents who is responsible for distributing their contents. The mailings include procedural information, informational data, and items for chapter action. A harassed chapter president, without the aid of carefully selected committees, may at times neglect to relay these data with their full content and intent to the chapter, hence an important breakdown in vital communications occurs. In such instances the chapter is out of touch with the program and policy of Grand Chapter. It has happened that the national office was not notified of a change of address or of the election of new officers, and subsequently an entire chapter became temporarily a closed circuit.

The lack of adequate committee function is borne out by statistics that report that 31 per cent of all chapters had no publicity and public relations committees; 55 per cent had no projects committee to implement Delta's public service program; and 37 per cent did not describe the function of the executive committee. The audit uncovered a major strength in chapter-to-individual relationships, weakened only by the malfunctioning committee networks.

To face these statistics honestly is to admit that a large percentage of Delta chapters are not sharing in Grand Chapter program. As a corollary, therefore, another major weakness on chapter level is chapter-to-public communication as it relates specifically to Delta program.

Today, approximately sixty-six times as many women finish college as did fifty years ago. In 1913, Delta membership represented approximately 11 per cent of the Negro women receiving degrees that year; today, approximately 22 per cent of the Negro women college graduates in any given year would represent Delta initiates. In fifty years Delta's growth has only doubled. This poses a serious problem. Ten years earlier the enrollment in a particular college was 2,000 and the probation line 20; why in 1960 was the probation line still 20, when the college enrollment had risen to 6,000?

Delta is hard at work to determine if such a growth rate is sufficient considering her scholastic standards, the number of chapters, and the selection procedure. The sorority derives its membership from the female college public. The responsibility for attracting new members is the local chapter's. Thus it is obvious that Grand Chapter must provide the local chapters with greater direction in this vital area.

Even more important than the drawing of new members into the ranks is the need for reclaiming Deltas who for one reason or another are inactive. Delta Sigma Theta is not proud of the fact that only 25 per cent of her membership is active and financial. In these Golden Anniversary years an intensive campaign is being conducted to reclaim the 24,000 "lost Deltas," most of whom are in the alumnae category. In a poll taken to determine why these Delta members had drifted away, the primary reasons listed for inactivity were: lack of finances, time, or interest, work obligations, other interests, and family obligations.

Not being able to afford Delta was the reason most often given by recent graduates, who indeed have the most valid claim to this position. Recent graduates represent, on an annual basis, the largest potential increase in Delta's active ranks as members of alumnae chapters. Alumnae dues are generally only slightly higher than those exacted from undergraduates, but it must be noted that, on local alumnae level, special activity taxes often accompany regular dues. Thus lack of finances probably is a major deterrent for the newly graduated Delta, who now may bear total responsibility to self-support.

The fact that many of these women voluntarily return to Delta after a few years in no way mitigates the constant gap created by the period of inactivity. No penalty is exacted for inactivity; for by reason of the oath taken at initiation, the sorority recognizes "once a Delta, always a Delta." Yet the active membership keenly feels the lack of these Deltas "on vacation."

It is hoped that the organization will find means of remedying this situation. It is probable, from the results of the Chapter Audit, that another telling factor here is that alumnae chapters do not provide a stimulation equivalent to that provided by the undergraduate chapter. Three- and four-hour-long meetings, however well-intentioned and organized, can tend to be tiring and tedious, particularly for those who fall into the age-bracket of the recent graduate.

Again, there is indication of a breakdown in communication from Grand Chapter to local chapter. The By-Laws clearly provide for a class of membership for persons who do not have the time for full participation. But only 14 per cent of Delta chapters have Members-at-Large. And, in answer to the audit questionnaire, only two chapters cited this membership category as a means of reclamation—a directive that has often been reiterated by Grand Chapter.

A less tangible factor, but one often cited, was the difference in age, education, experience, social and employment status that the recent graduate finds on entering an alumnae chapter. The most frequently mentioned difference was that of age. Yet, the youth-adult association is in essence the foundation of Delta structure; for here, hopefully, is the potential for union of the maturity gained from experience with the fresh and intrepid vision of the young.

The sorority as never before is aware of the need for strengthening its youth-adult relationships. The Chapter audit that has revealed the weaknesses may also point the way to determining avenues for correcting them.

The financing of the local program was also explored by the

Chapter Audit. Few local chapters are supported on dues exclusively, and money raising projects are varied. But a look at how the largest portions of the chapters' funds are spent underscores the realization that chapter emphases do not necessarily synchronize with those of the national body. As reported, 43 per cent of the chapters spend the largest portions of their budgets on traditional activities; 30 per cent spend the largest amount on social activities; 14 per cent spend the largest amount on contributions to other agencies and programs; and 13 per cent spend the largest amount on Delta projects.

Do these findings flatly contradict the image of public service that Delta Sigma Theta has been striving for so many years to create and maintain? To the degree that the public is impressed by Grand Chapter—its thinking, its goals, and its program—the answer will be no. But to the degree that the public is impressed by the thinking, goals, and program of the local chapter, the answer would appear to be sadly in the affirmative.

With the release of these statistics, a firm enjoinder was issued by Wilma H. Ray, recent Associate Director, whose responsibility it was to compile the data: "The public must not think of us as a schizophrenic organization, with a Grambling Conference getting major national emphasis, and a ticket for Little Miss Jabberwock getting the major emphasis in Ipswich."

All the facts revealed by the audit were not so discomfiting. While 45 per cent of Delta chapters have project committees, 95 per cent have social committees. But of these, 27 per cent report that social emphasis is increasing; 30 per cent say it is about the same; and 34 per cent say it is decreasing. The fact that social emphases *are* decreasing, however slowly, together with the fact that 64 per cent of the chapters feel that Delta's public image is and should be that of a public service organization, is the basis for some encouragement.

In an effort to prove this, many chapters, feeling the need to promote the serious aspects of Delta program, have discontinued the traditional and long-cherished Jabberwock, which is hardly more than an evening of sheer merriment. Yet, Grand Chapter is somewhat reluctant to frown officially on the Jabberwock, for it is clean entertainment, and 36 per cent of the chapters report it an effective way of raising money. What is more vital a concern is the use to which the money is put. In most instances the profit from the Jabberwock is used at least partially to support the chapter scholarship fund.

It is reported that 80 per cent of the chapters give scholarships ranging in amounts from $10 to $2,000. However, only 7 per cent of the chapters give scholarships which are sustained over a four-year period. Only in few instances were the criteria or the system for choosing recipients outlined. The listed criteria were scholarship, character, need, personality, and leadership ability. Of the recipients, 48 per cent remained in school and 10 per cent did not; 42 per cent of the chapters were unable to report about them. The values of giving scholarships seem to be primarily that in encouraging deserving and needy students and in getting chapter recognition in the community.

With regard to both the Jabberwock and the Scholarship Fund, Delta Sigma Theta is asking herself some probing questions. Is the Jabberwock the kind of activity in which so much Delta time, effort, and money should be invested? Is it relevant, in an atomic age, to the kind and caliber of public service the sorority is trying to render? If the purpose of the Jabberwock is to support scholarships, is Delta, even on local level, justified in this era in giving $25, $50, or $100 scholarships, which cannot possibly render any lasting or worth-while scholarship aid.

At the time when Delta began giving scholarships, financial aid to Negroes was very limited. This is no longer true, for not only are there many foundations for this purpose, but almost every other Negro organization has a scholarship program. Is this then, the best use for Delta money? Does giving a scholarship build Delta image in a community to the degree that a well-organized project would? In fact, does Delta at chapter level *give away too much money?*

Another area for Delta concern is the chapter implementation of the national projects. Twenty-eight per cent of the chapters have Job Opportunities Projects, 18 per cent have International Projects, 48 per cent have Mental Health Projects, 26 per cent have Library Projects, and 77 per cent have Volunteers for Community Service; 34 per cent work in only one project area, 31 per cent in two, 16 per cent in three, 9 per cent in four, and 1 per cent in all five. No report at all on projects was received from 19 per cent of the chapters.

As grave a matter for consideration were the reports of the caliber and degree of participation in the projects. For example, while a good number of chapters described in detail how they scheduled volunteer participation and listed the agencies with which they worked, many responded with, "We gave a radio to the mental hospital," or "We sent books and magazines to the children's home," and classified these activities as pertaining to volunteer, mental health, and library alike.

In her bulletin report, Program Assistant Wilma Ray questions: "Is this an adequate description of what we are trying to do? Does it give us a distinction from the ladies' aid society? Are we using our B-average mind to an advantage, or is it becoming a superfluous nicety to be used at rush parties and public meetings? These are the questions with which we must come to grip."

What is clarified as a result of the Chapter Audit? It would appear that in every area of concern there is one primary and identical need: Delta Sigma Theta must find and utilize ways by which every chapter, however remote, could be motivated, educated, and guided toward mastery of a more efficient administration unit, broadening its outlook, and directing its total program in keeping with the vision and goals of Grand Chapter.

It is an urgent and immediate demand. It is probable that additional staff eventually will be employed to serve as liaison field workers between local chapters and Grand Chapter. Whatever the solution, it must be found soon; for until this is done, Delta will not have come fully of age, nor will she be able fully to utilize her potential. For if Grand Chapter is the head of her organism, the local chapters are her arms and legs, her hands and feet, the constituents of her body and all its functions.

GOLDEN ANNIVERSARY—A MEANINGFUL PROCESS IN MOTION

Following the 1958 Convention, the Executive Board of Delta Sigma Theta Sorority authorized the appointment of a Golden Anniversary Committee. This committee, co-chaired by Past National President Dorothy I. Height and Gwendolyn Higginbotham, met in July of 1959 to begin to formulate initial plans. The committee outlined their goals:

> We must have a celebration worthy of all we hold dear. We must also discover:
>
> —how we can come to a deeper understanding of ourselves as Delta women;
>
> —how we can realize our mission as a Public Service Sorority in these changing times;
>
> —how we can strengthen our financial foundation and assure a greater future.

On the basis of these goals, the wheels of the Golden Anniversary were set in motion. To implement the first phase, coming to a "deeper understanding of ourselves as Delta women," the Yancey Commission and the Chapter Audit were initiated. To realize her mission as a public service sorority, Delta Sigma Theta had first to undergo a period of self-study. The second goal thus was contingent upon the first. But as soon as the Yancey and Audit reports began to clarify areas for development, Delta began to take meaningful steps to finding solutions.

If, as shown by the Chapter Audit, a major need was the redirecting of chapter program and thinking in line with that of the national body, the organization could hardly wait until such time as additional staff could be employed to do the job. Immediate moves had to be made.

With this in mind, National President Dr. Jeanne L. Noble, in December of 1961, called together a series of Officers Round Tables, held at various key sites throughout the country. Designed to be an intensive leadership workshop, the Officers Round Table was comprised of all local chapter officers, undergraduate advisors, and local Golden Anniversary Committees. Each Round Table was held within a three-hour traveling radius of each chapter, and serviced by national officers, national staff, and national committee personnel.

Comparing the Delta Round Table to that of King Arthur and his knights. Dr. Noble wrote in a letter to the sorority, published in the December, 1961, *Delta Journal,* immediately following the 35 conferences: "The [King Arthur's] Round Table was 'to represent a perfect world, where love and goodness would move in a power which would move out through every vein of life in Britain.' The agenda for our meetings gave equal time to human relations and public service skills. The roundness of King Arthur's table made all the knights an equal fellowship, none above or below, and none having a first or last seat. We met in an informal day of work, totally dedicated to sharing and learning . . . We hope that this experience will give us the inspiration to serve and lead the organization we love and to go the second mile."

The purposes of the Round Table were simple and definite: first, to help chapter leaders clarify and understand leadership roles and responsibilities, and second, to involve chapter leaders in setting goals and objectives for local chapter direction and achievement in the Golden Anniversary years.

As an outcome of these workshops, both alumnae and undergraduate chapter officers returned to their local chapters with definite plans and techniques for reaching specific goals. A booklet outlined ways and means to reach these goals:

1. *Membership:* To increase the active membership during next two years.
2. *Projects:* To strengthen the Five-Point Program.

3. *Program:* To upgrade the entire chapter program to reflect more accurately Delta purposes and training.
4. *Public Relations:* To establish and reinforce the image of Delta as that of a public service organization.
5. *Financial:* To assist in raising of a quarter of a million dollars by 1963, in order to advance Delta's Public Service Program and to endow her future.

Reclamation of inactive Deltas, a constant concern of the sorority and one urgent aspect of Membership, was now to become a concerted drive. Detailed suggestions for procedure were given, as they were for every objective. In the preceding year some strides had already been made in the area of reclamation. Under Geraldine P. Woods, Delta's First Vice-President, and Chairman of the Scholarship and Standards Committee, the local chapters had already reclaimed 900 members. The techniques employed included the use of the slogan, "Each One Reach One," the adoption as a pal of an inactive member by an active one, personal telephone calls and visits, the sharing of Delta publications and Delta experiences, the use of the Member-at-Large category, and the temporary waiving of national reinstatement fees.

Directives were also made by use of which chapters could close the transitional gap between undergraduate and alumnae affiliation. These included the planning of activities for newly graduated members by alumnae chapters, familiarizing such members with the chapter program, granting them equal responsibility in executing the Five-Point Program, and making chapter meetings more diversified and stimulating.

Undergraduate chapters were urged to develop new techniques of rushing, concentrating on personal contact and inclusive group activities; to increase initiations so that they reflect more accurately the increased college enrollment, and to make certain that every graduating Delta is referred to the alumnae chapter in the city in which she resides.

It is Delta's hope that with a unified, intensive program of reclamation, she may soon be able to cite the largest percentage of her 32,000 members as being active and financial.

It might be well to mention here the Delta Legacy, which covers one aspect of membership. A key to the virility of every organization is the pride its members take in being identified with it. Traditionally, fraternal organizations derive much of their membership from members of families. It is a healthy pride, and Delta encourages Deltas to pass on to their daughters and sisters the desire to be Deltas also. Such legatees make excellent Deltas, for they come to the sorority already equipped with the necessary values and spirit.

The use of committees was especially stressed at the Round Tables for the purpose of strengthening the Five-Point Program and of upgrading the entire chapter program.

In the area of public relations, alumnae chapters were directed to increase the visibility of the service projects, to develop at least one project to the degree that it would be immediately identifiable with the name Delta in the specific community, to concentrate on making the power structure of the community aware of Delta and Delta program; and especially to decrease the amount of press coverage of social activities which often in the past had served to outbalance the public service image.

Undergraduate chapters could also aid in building the public image by increasing the visibility of the service projects on campus, by maintaining a healthy relationship with other fraternal and campus organizations, by encouraging participation by Deltas in diverse activities, and matching every "queenship" with a position of leadership. (Deltas are noted for winning campus queen contests.)

The final objective listed in the Round Table handbook refers to the financial objective set by the Golden Anniversary Committee, to be realized by the 1963 National Convention. At the 1960 Convention, the Golden Anniversary Committee had presented and received approval for the following proposal:

> A financial campaign through which Delta Women and their families and friends contribute toward a GOLDEN ANNIVERSARY

> FUND, with a goal of a quarter of a million dollars by "sixty-three." The purpose of this year-by-year campaign will be to express appreciation, confidence, and hope in the past, present, and future of Delta Sigma Theta; to sustain and support an expanding program of scholarships and public service projects; and to build an endowment to ensure Delta's growth in the years to come.

To this purpose the year of 1959-1960 marked the introduction of the Golden Anniversary Gleaner, giving every Delta an opportunity to join with other members and friends in making a contribution to the Golden Anniversary Fund. Since then, every chapter has been engaged in activities to raise the "corporate gifts." Many gifts of $100 and more are being made by individual Deltas, known for that reason as Golden Anniversary Pioneers. Various fund-raising projects are currently striving toward acquiring the desired amount.

The goal of $250,000 was not arrived at haphazardly, and it was seen as being attainable in view of Delta's numbers and resources. It was also estimated in light of Delta's immediate and future economic needs. As an organization with growing numbers and program, Delta Sigma Theta has needed to expand both its staff and its Headquarters building. Consequently, additional staff has already been secured, and plans have been completed for an additional wing of the building in Washington, D.C.

Moreover, the time has come when the sorority must operate, as does "big business," on a well-padded financial base. Delta's income always has been erratic, because the organization derived support mainly from membership dues, the sum total of which rises or falls annually, depending upon the given membership in a particular year. And in ten years, despite the rising costs of living, Delta has not raised her national dues. The need for a more secure economic foundation is obvious.

It was recommended to the Golden Anniversary Committee by Delta's Public Relations Counsel that the fund-raising campaign be a continuous annual drive. The counsel also suggested that the Committee, in line with Delta's widening horizons, begin to set

Delta's sights on some bold goal in order firmly to promote the sorority's desired public image—the establishment in this country of a Delta Academy of Education for African Students, to be taught by qualified Delta women, thus furthering the International Project. Whether or not this proposal is accepted, it is reasonable to assume that Delta's program, if not widening in scope, will surely broaden in nature and degree, and that its implementation will require greater accumulated funds. Delta Sigma Theta, therefore, dedicates her corporate gift to the insuring of her future as a public service organization.

The Round Table was not the only tool to be utilized by the sorority to improve her total program in the Golden Anniversary years. It has been previously noted that Delta's pilot conferences for the Job Opportunities Project, held from time to time in each region, have evidenced among their end-rewards a strengthening of the Five-Point Project and the Delta image. Such a conference, titled "The Delta Workshop on Counseling Minority Youth," was co-sponsored by Delta Sigma Theta and the General Extension Division, Portland Center of the University of Oregon at Portland, and there conducted in June of 1961.

The theme, "Counseling Minority Youth," was explored by experts in guidance and psychiatry, and was offered to teachers, counselors, and volunteers on a credit and non-credit basis. The majority of the participants were non-Delta and a large percentage were white. It was intended that these would take new insights and knowledge back to their communities. And, since the workshop was held just prior to the 1961 Farwest Regional Conference, the Delta workshop participants were able to bring new information to the Regional Conference, to be disseminated to the Farwest chapters.

In her Golden Anniversary years, Delta Sigma Theta, an organization comprised largely of Negro women, with a major emphasis on youth in general and Negro youth in particular, has a continuous interest in the problems of minority youth. Kara V. Jackson, Chairman of Delta's National Projects Committee, and Director of Student Personnel and Guidance at Grambling College in Grambling,

Louisiana, delivered an address to the assembled Workshop in which she stated some of the problems confronting minority youth:

> "There are a half million children in the juvenile courts of America each year. Fifty per cent of our youth are dropping out of high school before graduating; eleven per cent of all young Americans are minority youth representing facets of the three races of mankind commonly referred to as the white, black, and yellow races. These youth are seriously impeded by race discrimination in their search for education, jobs, and housing. It is no secret that the majority of minority youth are reared in substandard housing and poverty, and come from broken homes. These figures represent an enormous waste of manpower and human potential which cause us dismay.
>
> "Can America, the land of equality, freedom, and justice, afford this waste of human potential in a world where a cold war, which may soon become hot, is being fought because these virtues are in conflict with another ideology? National status, in terms of equality of opportunity, seems basic to survival. As never before, our nation needs to motivate talent from three new sources: (1) lower economic groups, (2) Negroes, and (3) women. Eli Ginzberg says, in *The Negro Potential,* that the Negro is the most underdeveloped resource in the country. You will know, better than I, what other minority groups are failing, as the Negro, to motivate their children; to stimulate them to learn; to counsel them along the lines of making wise choices in planning their lives. . . ."

Mrs. Jackson then drew attention to the many phases of youth's behavior patterns, and explained that although minority youth is burdened with the problems common to all youth together with the problems peculiar to the discriminated-against minority, his needs are identical with those of all youngsters: to achieve, to be informed, to be loved and appreciated, to belong. She said further.

> "It seems appropriate to suggest that we are here to help our communities absorb minority groups. We are here to learn how to be friendly with these youngsters; to make them glad that they are alive and are our neighbors.

> "To summarize, I would say that the objectives of this conference could be stated in these terms: (1) It is imperative that communities, large and small throughout our nation should create and contrive a sense of order in dealing with problems of minority groups. This new sense of order provides an opportunity for the highest possible type of individual achievement; it establishes free and open communication among all of the racial groups in a community. (2) Those who work with minorities need to be fortified with the scientific facts about human nature; they need to turn these facts into very practical and everyday usage. (3) Specialized services in our communities, adapted to serve the individual's varied needs, will thrive in accordance with the understanding and support which people like us can give them."

The Workshop on Counseling Minority Youth was so well received in the northwest section of the country that it was repeated in 1962. Moreover, its success brought requests from other universities for similar demonstration projects.

Delta, in her workshops, has made a wise investment. As more and more chapters qualify to host such pilot projects, Delta's chances for foundation subsidy will be enhanced, and a happy by-product will be the establishment of her true public image. More important are the vast opportunities for service offered by these workshops.

Pilot projects are envisioned as a means of assisting chapters to increase their skills to the extent that they will be able to continue a project in a community after the pilot phase has passed. In a changing era when desegregation, actual or imminent, bewilders and disturbs the local community, such conferences can be the leaven that will sweeten and lighten the bitter bread of racial enmity and strife. In Delta's own ranks, armed with new approaches to the behavior of young people, Delta alumnae, advisors, and counselors will be able better to guide and direct the Delta undergraduate.

Delta publications have not been overlooked as a means toward reaching Golden Anniversary goals. The March, 1960, issue of the

Delta Newsletter, devoted completely to Golden Anniversary objectives, used two and a half of its four pages to introduce the Delta I.Q. or "I–Check"—a simple yes-no questionnaire designed for individual Delta self-appraisal. It was designed by Mrs. Helen F. Southard, Family Life Consultant, Leadership Services Department, National Board of the Y.W.C.A. Its purpose was to help each Delta come to a deeper realization of herself as a woman, and to evaluate the mission of the sorority in this era.

In succeeding issues of the *Newsletter,* other "I–Checks" have been issued to appraise individual knowledge of the sorority, its structure and policy.

The informal self-studies, in their challenging quiz form, have served to spur Deltas, especially undergraduates, to discover and correct errors in their own thinking. The *Newsletter* also has served the purpose of guidance. A four-page "slick" publication, it is more assuredly read from cover to cover by undergraduates than the larger *Delta Journal.* With its informal bulletin style, it can and does serve a unique purpose, for various and sundry bits of Golden Anniversary information and directions find their way into its pages and sly cartoons give pointed Delta messages. In an open letter to undergraduates, the Program Assistant, Wilma H. Ray, raised some pointed questions about initiation practices. Hazing, while officially banned by Grand Chapter has still not been abolished by all chapters, as case studies made during the preceding years have shown. In some cases the letter of the law is strictly obeyed, while the spirit is freely violated. The sorority feels that a wound to the human psyche is even more deplorable than one to the body.

To this point, in the January, 1961 *Newsletter,* Wilma Ray asks:

> *Who are we?* Are we young women who invite other young women with intellectual and creative abilities to join our ranks so that we can subjugate them to all manner of indignities and inconsiderations?
> *What are we?* Are we an association of proud, but aging, adolescents, who feel that we have so much to offer that we sit smugly,

> basking in past glory, while the very character of the world changes before our eyes, unnoticed?
> *Why are we?* Do we exist on the premise that ours is a provincial and microcosmic organizational world, having the unique ability of transposing months of subservience into immediate sisterliness and service with one ceremony?
>
> Having documented what are are not, you can evolve the real who, what, and why of our being. As we consider these questions, let us never weigh outmoded tradition above an honest need for change, substitute frivolity for wholesome fellowship, or become so engrossed in our local activities that we lose sight of our larger program and goals.

The *Delta Journal,* on the other hand, has devoted itself during this period to articles of pertinent social, civic, and political interest. Prominent people in various walks of life have made contributions. The May, 1962, *Journal* features an article entitled, "What You Can Do For Your Country," by Mrs. Margaret Price, Vice-Chairman of the Democratic National Committee; on the opposite page is featured an article, "Women Help Us Keep the Two-Party System," by Mrs. Clara B. Williams, the Assistant Chairman of the Republican National Committee. In the same issue, J. B. Jones, Associate Dean of Students at Texas Southern University, has contributed an article about self-overvaluation entitled, "How Big Am I?" It is articles like these that enable Deltas to widen their horizons and better envision Delta goals and program as they relate to the world.

To what does it all add up? This probing self-evaluation, this avid concern for self-improvement? In a speech to the 1959 Regional Conferences, National President Dr. Jeanne L. Noble stated it simply: "The Bible says, 'Where there is no vision, the people perish. But he that keepeth the law, happy is he.' What is the law? In these days of changing patterns when many people seriously question the purpose of a sorority, I still believe that Delta Sigma Theta has a responsible law, and thus a right to a place in the future. It was clear in 1913; it is clear today. *The mission of Delta Sigma Theta is to educate and project the skills, understanding, and resources of its members for community service.* It is a simple law, and yet it bespeaks a profound mission. Without it we perish."

THE GOLDEN ANNIVERSARY

The Fiftieth Anniversary Birthday Celebration of Delta Sigma Theta Sorority was held in Washington, D.C. on January 12 and 13, 1963. There, at the historic site of Delta's founding, 400 Deltas from numerous cities met to pay homage to Delta's Founders, and to rededicate themselves to those ideals and purposes which are Delta's spark of life. Indeed, the hearts of Deltas everywhere turned in a voluntary pilgrimage of devotion to that spot where fifty years earlier, twenty-two young women had conceived those ideals and purposes.

The Golden Anniversary Luncheon, held on January 12, in the Senate Room of Washington's International Inn, was an occasion made memorable by the presence of the President of the United States, John F. Kennedy. In his remarks to those assembled, President Kennedy said that he wished, "to express my best wishes to you all and express my admiration to you as President for your services to the country. . . . A free society," he said, "places greater burdens upon its citizens than any other kind of system." He commended the sorority for her efforts in the area of education, emphasizing the fact that there is a need for a larger concern on the part of the American people: ". . . those who have talent should have the opportunity to develop it. That's what the essence of freedom is! . . . I think that all of us will say that there's a great deal left undone, and to the finishing of these tasks we commit ourselves."

The Honorable Edith Green, United States Representative from the Third Congressional District of Oregon, delivered the main luncheon address. Discussing education and equal opportunity for all, Mrs. Green said, "The community, the state, the nation so desperately need talented trained people. . . . Now we are literally and physically reaching for the stars. Those who cannot, or will not, stay abreast of these new developments will find that not the world, but the universe will pass them by. . . . Today, more desperately than anything else, we need to build not just pathways to the stars, but bridges of understanding—first, here at home among our own people, and then, bridges of understanding to the people of other parts of the world."

Many distinguished women attended this Golden Anniversary Luncheon, paying tribute by their presence to Delta Sigma Theta's fifty years of service. Special guests included Mrs. S. Edward Peal, wife of the Ambassador of Liberia; Mrs. J. Edward Day, wife of the Postmaster General; Mrs. Luther Hodges, wife of the Secretary of Commerce; Mrs. W. Willard Wirtz, wife of the Secretary of Labor; Mrs. Chester Bowles, wife of the Special Advisor to the President on African, Asian, and Latin American Affairs; Mrs. G. Mennon Williams, wife of the Assistant Secretary of State for African Affairs; Mrs. Pedro A. Sanjuan, wife of the Deputy Chief of Protocol; Mrs. Esther Peterson, Assistant Secretary of Labor; Mrs. Katie Loucheim, Deputy Secretary for Public Affairs; and Mrs. James Nabritt, wife of the President of Howard University.

The purpose of the Golden Anniversary Luncheon was made especially meaningful by the presence of the ten Founders: Winona Cargile Alexander, Osceola McCarthy Adams, Ethel Cuff Black, Bertha Pitts Campbell, Myra Davis Hemmings, Jimmie Bugg Middleton, Eliza P. Shippen, Florence Letcher Toms, Wertie Blackwell Weaver, and Madree Penn White.

Each Founder was introduced to the assembly and spoke briefly, commending the sorority for her achievements of the past and expressing confidence in her future. These were among the women who had banded together, 50 years earlier, for the purpose of public service, an ideal that had drawn to it thousands of women across the nation and in other parts of the world. It was fitting that these Founders were honored at such an occasion, and later on the following day at a reception attended by such dignitaries as Lyndon B. Johnson, then Vice-President of the United States, and William O. Douglas, Associate Justice of the Supreme Court.

The Vice-President, emphasizing the privileged economic position of the United States and its need to extend its privileges to all its citizens, said, "Until justice is blind to color, until education is unaware of race, until opportunity ceases to squint its eyes at pigmentation of human complexion, emancipation will be a proclamation, but it will not be a fact. So we have a lot of work cut out for us. . . . We're going to continue to move forward."

Justice Douglas affirmed the thought by saying, "This appetite for knowledge, this desire to learn is deep in all people; and nobody, no race, no one nation has a monopoly on genius and talent. That's why this thing that you're doing, making educational opportunities available to those who otherwise wouldn't have them, is the great thing. . . ."

The Golden Anniversary Celebration was more than a loving salute to the Founders, and more than a commemoration of past achievements. It was, as every Founder and every speaker pointed out in several ways, "a time for new beginnings." It was in this understanding that Delta chose as its fiftieth anniversary theme: "The Past is Prologue." It was for this reason that the two-day celebration ended in an almost tangible spirit of anticipation. It was probably this same spirit that prompted Justice Douglas, as he closed his remarks to the sorority, to utilize the words a taxi driver has once spoken to him: "I move that you adopt as your motto, 'You ain't seen nothing yet!' "

AND NOW TOMORROW

In August of 1963, a thousand Deltas convened at the Americana Hotel in New York City for the 27th National Convention of Delta Sigma Theta Sorority. This was the Golden Jubilee Convention, and what was proposed and resolved reflected the same spirit of preparation with which the Founders, fifty years before, inaugurated the sorority. It was a time for serious and careful planning, and for thoughtful analysis of the sorority's role in the present and the future; for Delta Sigma Theta could not help but be reminded that her Fiftieth Anniversary coincided with the Centennial Anniversary of the Emancipation Proclamation.

One hundred years before, Abraham Lincoln issued the Proclamation that emancipated from slavery the forebears of the large majority of Delta's members. To those ancestors—who as freed slaves bore that period of turmoil and bewilderment while endeavoring to point the way for future generations—Delta must also bear a duty and a dedication. The Delta torch, reminding each member of her mission to enlighten, to ennoble, and to uplift wherever possible, was lighted long before the twenty-two beloved Founders conceived the Delta ideal. It has burned in the hearts of right-thinking men and women throughout the ages, for it is the ever-brightening torch of loving service, of freedom and truth, that has led mankind from primeval slime to outer space; and which, hopefully, will lead him higher through the ages yet to come.

Delta Sigma Theta, gratefully honoring her past at her half-century milestone and honestly appraising her present, has no real fear for her future. That she has made and will make mistakes is natural to her human composition. That she will always seek to remedy her errors, to uplift herself, to serve her community, and therefore continuously to fulfill her mission, is her faith. In the ranks of her undergraduates are hundreds of Freedom Fighters, with the same bold, courageous, visionary spirit of the suffragette Founders. The sorority does not fear that they will fail their mission as Deltas. The seeds of integrity, scholarship, service, and progress, planted by young women fifty years ago and flourishing now as the Delta tree, were well sown. As the organization faces the future, even as new seeds are planted, it does not in truth matter if fifty years hence Delta Sigma Theta will exist by her present name and in her present form. What does matter, is that in the forest of human endeavor, if the Delta ideal has been nobly perpetuated and has spread itself abroad ever to widen and deepen its sphere of influence, then—in whatever shape or form, by whatever name—the tree will endure.

Appendix A Founders

Osceola McCarthy Adams
Marguerite Young Alexander*
Winona Cargile Alexander
Ethel Cuff Black
Bertha Pitts Campbell
Zephyr J. Chisom Carter
Edna Brown Coleman*
Jessie McGuire Dent*
Fredericka Chase Dodd
Myra Davis Hemmings
Olive Jones*

Jimmie Bugg Middleton
Pauline Oberdorfer Minor*
Vashti Turley Murphy*
Naomi Sewell Richardson
Mamie Reddy Rose*
Eliza P. Shippen
Florence Letcher Toms
Ethel Carr Watson*
Wertie Blackwell Weaver
Madree Penn White
Edith Motte Young

* Deceased

Appendix B Honorary Members

Daisy Bates
Madeleine Sylvain Bouchereau
Mary Cromwell
Christine Ray Davis
Sadie Overton Davis
Edith Green
Effie Grant Hardy
Lena Horne
Rowena Jelliffe
Daisy E. Lampkin
India Maxwell
Eunice H. Nelson
Camille Nickerson
Marjorie Penny
Anna Grace Sawyer
Philippa Schuyler
Dorothy Tilley
Nannie M. Turner
Mary Elizabeth Vroman
Estelle Pinckney Webster
Gertrude Woodward

DECEASED

Mary McCleod Bethune
Hallie Quinn Brown
Nannie Burroughs
Coralie F. Cook
Fannie Emanuel
Laura B. Glenn
Geraldine Green
Cecilia Gregg
Jessie Faucett Harris
Anna Hughes
Julia Gee Hunnicut
Florence Cole McCleave
Melvina Mitchell
Alice Dunbar Nelson
Gabriel Pelham
Gertrude D. Rush
Sarah Scarborough
Frankie Talbert
Mary Church Terrell
Mary Fitzbutler Waring
Josephine Washington
Margaret Murray Washington
D. A. Whittaker

Appendix C National Presidents and terms of office

Sadie T. M. Alexander	1919–1923
Dorothy Pelham Beckley**	1923–1926
Ethel Lamay Calimese**	1926–1929
Anna Johnson Julian	1929–1931
Gladys Byram Shepperd	1931–1933
Jeannette Tripplett Jones**	1933–1935
Vivian Osborne Marsh	1935–1939
Elsie Austin	1939–1944
Mae Wright Peck	1944–1947
Dorothy I. Height	1947–1956
Dorothy P. Harrison	1956–1958
Jeanne L. Noble	1958–1963

** Deceased

Appendix D National conventions

1st.	December 27, 1919	Howard University, Washington, D. C. *Three of existing five chapters present. Plans made to nationalize.
2nd.	December 28, 1920	Wilberforce University, Wilberforce, Ohio. *Convention authorized *The Delta Journal;* Honorary Members; The Delta May Week and its slogan, "Invest in Education"; and Alumnae Chapters.
3rd.	December 31, 1921	University of Pennsylvania, Philadelphia, Pennsylvania. *Committee on Standards appointed, also Committee on Scholastic Grades.
4th.	December, 1922	Chicago, Illinois. *Convention authorized a Scholarship Award Fund and a College Tuition Loan Fund.
5th.	December 27–30, 1923	Columbus, Ohio. *Honorary membership accorded Mary M. Bethune.
6th.	December 27, 1924	New York City. *Delta Sigma Theta Hymn adopted.
7th.	December 27–31, 1924	Des Moines, Iowa. *Regional Conferences established. Revision of nomenclature for chapters.
8th.	December, 1926	Cincinnati, Ohio. *First drive against inactivity in chapters.

* Significant outcomes

9th.	December, 1927	Washington, D. C. *Strengthened program. Appointment of a National Vigilance Committee.
10th.	December 27, 1929	Pittsburgh, Pennsylvania. *The First Biennial Convention. Policies set for internal organization.
11th.	December 28, 1931	Nashville, Tennessee. *First mixed Chapter authorized.
12th.	August 27, 1933	Chicago, Illinois. *Increased concern for standards. "B" rated schools accepted for Delta.
13th.	August 10–15, 1935	Los Angeles, California. *Office of Executive Secretary created, not to be filled for some time.
14th.	December 27–31, 1937	Cleveland, Ohio. *Much dissension about internal affairs.
15th.	August 28–31, 1939	New York City. *114 chapters represented. All chapters required to take membership in NAACP. More support enlisted for Urban League. National officers cautioned to report only "facts," not "sentiment."
16th.	December 26–30, 1941	Detroit, Michigan. *Grand President delivered address on "Social Maturity." Mary Bethune pointed to the need for Delta service in the war crisis. Particular stress on the service programs.
17th.	August 24–27, 1944	Wilberforce University, Wilberforce, Ohio. *Convention was a year late because of war emergency. Petition was made by undergraduates to be represented on Executive Board. Gloria Hewlett was chosen as the first undergraduate Second Vice-President.
18th.	December 27–30, 1945	Richmond, Virginia. *First Convention with a theme: "Design for Living in a New Age." Much concern for the Delta program.
19th.	December 27–31, 1947	San Antonio, Texas. *Resolution to call on Congress to admit to the U.S. 100,000 selected refugees and displaced per-

* Significant outcomes

		sons for the next four years in addition to the regular quota. Formal adoption and copyright of the name Jabberwock.
20th.	August 23–28, 1948	St. Louis, Missouri. *Resolution to admit any qualified woman to Delta Sigma Theta, regardless of race, creed, or nationality. Creation of a Public Relations Board.
21st.	August 15–19, 1950	University of California at Berkeley. *Theme: "Human Rights, from Charter to Practice." Workshops geared to theme.
22nd.	December 26–31, 1952	Cleveland, Ohio. *Establishment of a National Headquarters. Reorganization of modus operandi—therefore called: The Mending Conference. The position of Executive Director now approved.
23rd.	August 14–20, 1954	New York City. *Concern for undergraduate status and problems. The "blackball" abolished.
24th.	December 26–30, 1956	Detroit, Michigan. *Theme: "Windows on the World." Revision of nomenclature. Graduate chapters thereafter to be known as alumnae chapters. The Member-at-Large category proposed.
25th.	August 17–23, 1958	Washington, D. C. *Theme: "The Challenge of Changing Patterns." An evaluating of the past and planning for the future. Plans made for the Golden Anniversary Period. The Member-at-Large category adopted.
26th.	August 14–21, 1960	Chicago, Illinois. *Theme: "The Creative Life in Freedom and Dignity." Resolution to complete the Maternity Wing of the Chania Medical Center in Kenya, West Africa. Resolution to support the stand taken by young Negro Americans to secure equal rights.
27th.	August 11–17, 1963	New York City. *THE GOLDEN ANNIVERSARY JUBILEE.

* Significant outcomes

Appendix E   Chapters and dates of establishment

Roster of Chapters—1963

ALUMNAE CHAPTERS

Chapter	*Former Name*	*Location*	*Region*	*Established*
Aiken-Augusta Alumnae	Delta Rho Sigma	Aiken, S. C.	SA	1952
Akron-Canton Alumnae	—	Akron, Ohio	MW	1960
Alaska Alumnae	—	Alaska	FW	1959
Albany Alumnae	Gamma Psi Sigma	Albany, Ga.	S	1948
Alcorn-Natchez Alumnae	—	Natchez, Miss.	S	1959
Alexandria Alumnae	Epsilon Theta Sigma	Alexandria, La.	SW	1955
Alexandria Alumnae	—	Alexandria, Va.	SA	1959
Amarillo Alumnae	—	Amarillo, Texas	SW	1962
Annapolis Alumnae	Gamma Omicron Sigma	Annapolis, Md.	E	1947
Ann Arbor Alumnae	—	Ann Arbor, Mich.	MW	1962
Ardmore Alumnae	Alpha Psi Sigma	Ardmore, Okla.	C	1949
Asheville Alumnae	Epsilon Lambda Sigma	Asheville, N. C.	SA	1955
Atlanta Alumnae	Iota Sigma	Atlanta, Ga.	S	1925
Austin Alumnae	Sigma Sigma	Austin, Texas	SW	1934
Baltimore Alumnae	Epsilon Sigma	Baltimore, Md.	E	1932
Baton Rouge Delta Alumnae	Upsilon Sigma	Baton Rouge, La.	SW	1932

Baton Rouge Sigma Alumnae	Epsilon Xi Sigma	Baton Rouge, La.	SW	1956
Beaumont Alumnae	Beta Nu Sigma	Beaumont, Texas	SW	1942
Beckley Alumnae	Beta Chi Sigma	Beckley, W. Va.	MW	1945
Berkeley Alumnae	Omega Sigma	Berkeley, Calif.	FW	1921
Birmingham Alumnae	Tau Sigma	Birmingham, Ala.	S	1931
Bluefield Alumnae	Alpha Epsilon Sigma	Bluefield, W. Va.	MW	1936
Boston Alumnae	Alpha Omicron Sigma	Boston, Mass.	E	1945
Brooklyn Alumnae	Delta Gamma Sigma	Brooklyn, N. Y.	E	1949
Broward County Alumnae	Epsilon Nu Sigma	Broward County, Fla.	S	1955
Brunswick Alumnae	—	Brunswick, Ga.	S	1958
Cambridge Alumnae	Delta Pi Sigma	Cambridge, Md.	E	1952
Charleston Alumnae	Beta Alpha Sigma	Charleston, S. C.	SA	1940
Charleston-Institute Alumnae	Phi Sigma	Institute, W. Va.	MW	1932
Charlotte Alumnae	Beta Xi Sigma	Charlotte, N. C.	SA	1942
Chattanooga Alumnae	Beta Epsilon	Chattanooga, Tenn.	S	1941
Chicago Alumnae	Theta Sigma	Chicago, Ill.	MW	1925
Cincinnati Alumnae	Beta Psi Sigma	Cincinnati, Ohio	MW	1945
Coffeyville Alumnae	Epsilon Zeta Sigma	Coffeyville, Kansas	C	1954
Columbia Alumnae	Beta Beta Sigma	Columbia, S. C.	SA	1940
Columbus Alumnae	Gamma Rho Sigma	Columbus, Ga.	S	1948
Columbus Alumnae	Alpha Beta Sigma	Columbus, Ohio.	MW	1932
Dallas Alumnae	Beta Delta	Dallas, Texas	SW	1926
Danville Alumnae	Gamma Gamma Sigma	Danville, Va.	SA	1946
Dayton Alumnae	Alpha Delta Sigma	Dayton, Ohio	MW	1936
Daytona Beach Alumnae	Gamma Zeta Sigma	Daytona Beach, Fla.	S	1946
Detroit Alumnae	Alpha Pi Sigma	Detroit, Mich.	MW	1939

Dover Alumnae	Epsilon Kappa Sigma	Dover, Delaware	E	1955
Durham Alumnae	Alpha Kappa Sigma	Durham, N. C.	SA	1941
East St. Louis Alumnae	—	E. St. Louis, Ill.	MW	1958
Elizabeth City Alumnae	Epsilon Beta Sigma	Elizabeth City, N. C.	SA	1953
Fayetteville Alumnae	Epsilon Alpha Sigma	Fayetteville, N. C.	SA	1953
Flint Alumnae	Epsilon Epsilon Sigma	Flint, Mich.	MW	1954
Florence Alumnae	Delta Omicron Sigma	Florence, S. C.	SA	1952
Fort Pierce Alumnae	—	Fort Pierce, Fla.	S	1960
Fort Valley Alumnae	Beta Omicron Sigma	Fort Valley, Ga.	S	1943
Frankfort Alumnae	Beta Upsilon Sigma	Frankfort, Ky.	MW	1944
Gastonia Alumnae	Delta Psi Sigma	Gastonia, N. C.	SA	1954
Grambling Alumnae	Gamma Upsilon Sigma	Grambling, La.	SW	1948
Greensboro Alumnae	Beta Nu Sigma	Greensboro, N. C.	SA	1942
Greenville Alumnae	—	Greenville, S. C.	SA	1962
Greenwood/Itta Bena Alumnae	—	Itta Bena, Miss.	S	1963
Hampton Alumnae	Delta Iota Sigma	Hampton, Va.	SA	1951
Harrisburg Alumnae	Epsilon Pi Sigma	Harrisburg, Pa.	E	1958
Hartford Alumnae	Gamma Nu Sigma	Hartford, Conn.	E	1947
Hayti Alumnae	Epsilon Tau Sigma	Hayti, Mo.	C	1958
High Point Alumnae	Alpha Omega Sigma	High Point, N. C.	SA	1949
Houston Alumnae	Delta Beta Sigma	Houston, Texas	SW	1949
Huntsville Alumnae	Epsilon Delta Sigma	Huntsville, Ala.	S	1954
Inkster Alumnae	—	Inkster, Mich.	MW	1959
Jackson Alumnae	Alpha Chi Sigma	Jackson, Miss.	S	1941
Jackson Alumnae	Beta Omega Sigma	Jackson, Tenn.	S	1945
Jacksonville Alumnae	Alpha Iota Sigma	Jacksonville, Fla.	S	1937

Jefferson City Alumnae	Alpha Upsilon Sigma	Jefferson City, Mo.	C	1939
Kinston Alumnae	—	Kinston, N. C.	SA	1958
Knoxville Alumnae	Gamma Theta Sigma	Knoxville, Tenn.	S	1947
Lake Charles Alumnae	Epsilon Eta Sigma	Lake Charles, La.	SW	1955
LaMarque Alumnae	—	LaMarque, Texas	SW	1961
Langston Alumnae	Beta Iota Sigma	Langston, Okla.	C	1940
Lansing Alumnae	—	Lansing, Mich.	MW	1960
Lawrenceville Alumnae	Delta Kappa Sigma	Lawrenceville, Va.	SA	1951
Lawton Alumnae	Beta Kappa Sigma	Lawton, Okla.	C	1942
Lexington Alumnae	Chi Sigma	Lexington, Ky.	MW	1932
Lexington Alumnae	Delta Eta Sigma	Lexington, Va.	SA	1951
Liberia Alumnae	—	Monrovia, Liberia	Foreign	1959
Little Rock Alumnae	Delta Epsilon Sigma	Little Rock, Ark.	SW	1950
Logan Alumnae	Delta Mu Sigma	Logan, W. Va.	MW	1952
Los Angeles Alumnae	Nu Sigma	Los Angeles, Calif.	FW	1934
Louisville Alumnae	Alpha Alpha Sigma	Louisville, Ky.	MW	1933
Lubbock Alumnae	Delta Xi Sigma	Lubbock, Texas	SW	1952
Lynchburg Alumnae	Alpha Theta Sigma	Lynchburg, Va.	SA	1939
Macon Alumnae	—	Macon, Ga.	S	1958
Marlin Alumnae	—	Marlin, Texas	SW	1962
Marshall Alumnae	Beta Tau Sigma	Marshall, Texas	SW	1939
Memphis Alumnae	Alpha Gamma Sigma	Memphis, Tenn.	S	1935
Miami Alumnae	Beta Zeta Sigma	Miami, Fla.	S	1941
Minden Alumnae	—	Minden, La.	SW	1960
Mobile Alumnae	Beta Eta Sigma	Mobile, Ala.	S	1942

Monroe Alumnae	Epsilon Iota Sigma	Monroe, La.	SW	1955
Montclair Alumnae	—	Montclair, N. J.	E	1962
Montgomery Alumnae	Alpha Lambda Sigma	Montgomery, Ala.	S	1937
Muskogee Alumnae	Alpha Rho Sigma	Muskogee, Okla.	C	1949
Nashville Alumnae	Pi Sigma	Nashville, Tenn.	S	1932
Nassau Alumnae	—	Nassau County, N. Y.	E	1963
New Bern Alumnae	Delta Chi Sigma	New Bern, N. C.	SA	1952
New Haven Alumnae	—	New Haven, Conn.	E	1959
New Iberia Alumnae	—	New Iberia, La.	SW	1962
New Orleans Alumnae	Alpha Eta Sigma	New Orleans, La.	SW	1936
Newport News Alumnae	Gamma Iota Sigma	Newport News, Va.	SA	1947
New York Alumnae	Alpha Sigma	New York, N. Y.	E	1920
Norfolk Alumnae	Mu Sigma	Norfolk, Va.	SA	1933
North Jersey Alumnae	Kappa Sigma	New Jersey	E	1939
Ocala Alumnae	—	Ocala, Fla.	S	1961
Odessa Alumnae	—	Odessa, Texas	SW	1964
Oklahoma City Alumnae	Eta Sigma	Oklahoma City, Okla.	C	1938
Okmulgee Alumnae	Beta Lambda Sigma	Okmulgee, Okla.	C	1942
Orange Alumnae	Delta Omega Sigma	Orange, Texas	SW	1953
Orangeburg Alumnae	Alpha Tau Sigma	Orangeburg, S. C.	SA	1939
Orlando Alumnae	Epsilon Gamma Sigma	Orlando, Fla.	S	1954
Oxford-Henderson Alumnae	Gamma Beta Sigma	Oxford, N. C.	SA	1945
Pasadena Alumnae	—	Pasadena, Calif.	FW	1961
Pensacola Alumnae	Delta Alpha Sigma	Pensacola, Fla.	S	1949
Petersburg Alumnae	Beta Gamma Sigma	Petersburg, Va.	SA	1941
Philadelphia Alumnae	Xi Sigma	Philadelphia, Pa.	E	1927

Pine Bluff Alumnae	Beta Phi Sigma	Pine Bluff, Ark.	SW	1944
Port Arthur Alumnae	Beta Sigma Sigma	Port Arthur, Texas	SW	1947
Port au Prince Alumnae	Delta Zeta Sigma	Port au Prince, Haiti.	Foreign	1950
Portsmouth Alumnae	Beta Pi Sigma	Portsmouth, Va.	SA	1943
Prairie View Alumnae	Delta Nu Sigma	Prairie View, Texas	SW	1952
Queens Alumnae	Delta Theta Sigma	Queens, New York	E	1951
Raleigh Alumnae	Alpha Zeta Sigma	Raleigh, N. C.	SA	1938
Richmond Alumnae	Beta Theta Sigma	Richmond, Va.	SA	1942
Roanoke Alumnae	Alpha Mu Sigma	Roanoke, Va.	SA	1939
Rock Hill Alumnae	Epsilon Rho Sigma	Rock Hill, S. C.	SA	1958
Rocky Mount Alumnae	Gamma Kappa Sigma	Rocky Mount, N. C.	SA	1947
St. Joseph Alumnae	Alpha Sigma Sigma	St. Joseph, Mo.	C	1939
St. Louis Alumnae	Lambda Sigma	St. Louis, Mo.	C	1926
St. Petersburg Alumnae	Gamma Mu Sigma	St. Petersburg, Fla.	S	1946
Salisbury Alumnae	Delta Tau Sigma	Salisbury, N. C.	SA	1952
San Antonio Alumnae	Psi Sigma	San Antonio, Texas	SW	1933
San Bernadino Alumnae	—	San Bernadino, Calif.	FW	1959
San Francisco Alumnae	Gamma Phi Sigma	San Francisco, Calif.	FW	1948
Savannah Alumnae	Beta Delta Sigma	Savannah, Ga.	S	1941
Selma Alumnae	Delta Upsilon Sigma	Selma, Ala.	S	1953
Sequin Alumnae	Gamma Sigma Sigma	Sequin, Texas	SW	1948
Shreveport Alumnae	Rho Sigma	Shreveport, La.	SW	1932
South Bend Alumnae	Epsilon Mu Sigma	South Bend, Ind.	MW	1955
Spartanburg Alumnae	Gamma Lambda Sigma	Spartanburg, S. C.	SA	1946
Suffolk Alumnae	—	Suffolk, Virginia	SA	1964
Sumter Alumnae	Gamma Xi Sigma	Sumter, S. C.	SA	1947

Tallahassee Alumnae	Gamma Eta Sigma	Tallahassee, Fla.	S	1946
Tampa Alumnae	—	Tampa, Fla.	S	1959
Temple Alumnae	Gamma Alpha Sigma	Temple, Texas	SW	1945
Trenton Alumnae	Delta Sigma Sigma	Trenton, N. J.	E	1952
Tulsa Alumnae	Omicron Sigma	Tulsa, Okla.	C	1930
Tuscaloosa Alumnae	Delta Delta Sigma	Tuscaloosa, Ala.	S	1950
Tuskegee Alumnae	Zeta Sigma	Tuskegee Institute, Ala.	S	1933
Tyler Alumnae	Gamma Epsilon Sigma	Tyler, Texas	SW	1946
Waco Alumnae	Beta Rho Sigma	Waco, Texas	SW	1944
Washington Alumnae	Beta Sigma	Washington, D. C.	E	1932
Westchester County Alumnae	—	Westchester County, N. Y.	E	1959
West Palm Beach Alumnae	Gamma Pi Sigma	West Palm Beach, Fla.	S	1948
Wewoka Alumnae	Alpha Xi Sigma	Wewoka, Oklahoma	C	1939
Wilberforce Alumnae	Delta Sigma	Wilberforce, Ohio	MW	1936
Wilmington Alumnae	Gamma Omega Sigma	Wilmington, Del.	E	1949
Wilmington Alumnae	Alpha Phi Sigma	Wilmington, N. C.	SA	1940
Wilson Alumnae	Epsilon Omicron Sigma	Wilson, N. C.	SA	1956
Winston-Salem Alumnae	Alpha Nu Sigma	Winston-Salem, N. C.	SA	1939

UNDERGRADUATE CHAPTERS

Chapter	*College*	*Location*	*Region*	*Estab-lished*
Alpha	Howard University	Washington, D. C.	E	1913
Alpha Beta	Fisk University	Nashville, Tenn.	S	1926
Alpha Chi	Tennessee State University	Nashville, Tenn.	S	1936
Alpha Delta	W. Virginia State College	Institute, West Virginia	MW	1926
Alpha Eta	Virginia State College	Petersburg, Virginia	SA	1929
Alpha Gamma	Morgan State College	Baltimore, Maryland	E	1926
Alpha Iota	Wiley College	Marshall, Texas	SW	1930
Alpha Kappa	Huston-Tillotson College	Austin, Texas	SW	1928
Alpha Lambda	North Carolina College	Durham, North Carolina	SA	1941
Alpha Mu	A & T College	Greensboro, N. C.	SA	1932
Alpha Nu	University of Illinois	Urbana, Illinois	MW	1932
Alpha Omega	Harris Teachers College	St. Louis, Missouri	C	1926
Alphi Pi	Kentucky State College	Frankfort, Kentucky	MW	1930
Alpha Rho	Shaw University	Raleigh, North Carolina	SA	1934
Alpha Tau	Southern University	Baton Rouge, Louisiana	SW	1934
Alpha Theta	Lincoln University	Jefferson City, Missouri	C	1930
Alpha Upsilon	Le Moyne College	Memphis, Tennessee	S	1927
Alpha Xi	S. C. State College	Orangeburg, S. C.	SA	1934

Alpha Zeta	Talladega College	Talladega, Alabama	S	1928
Beta	Wilberforce University	Wilberforce, Ohio	MW	1914
Beta Alpha	Fla. A & M University	Tallahassee, Florida	S	1936
Beta Chi	Lane College	Jackson, Tennessee	S	1939
Beta Epsilon	Virginia Union University	Richmond, Virginia	SA	1935
Beta Eta	Alabama State College	Montgomery, Alabama	S	1937
Beta Gamma	Dillard University	New Orleans, Louisiana	SW	1934
Beta Iota	D. C. Teachers College	Washington, D. C.	E	1937
Beta Kappa	Livingstone College	Salisbury, North Carolina	SA	1947
Beta Pi	Bluefield State College	Bluefield, West Virginia	MW	1936
Beta Upsilon	Langston University	Langston, Oklahoma	C	1938
Delta Alpha	Bethune-Cookman College	Daytona Beach, Florida	S	1949
Delta Beta	Eastern Michigan Univ.	Ypsilanti, Michigan	MW	1949
Delta Chi	State Teachers College	Elizabeth City, N. C.	SA	1953
Delta Delta	Alabama A & M College	Normal, Alabama	S	1949
Delta Epsilon	Alcorn A & M College	Lorman, Mississippi	S	1949
Delta Eta	A. M. & N. College	Pine Bluff, Arkansas	SW	1950
Delta Gamma	Texas Southern University	Houston, Texas	SW	1949
Delta Iota	Grambling College	Grambling, Louisiana	SW	1950
Delta Kappa	Central State College	Wilberforce, Ohio	MW	1951
Delta Mu	Maryland State College	Princess Anne, Maryland	E	1952
Delta Nu	Savannah State College	Savannah, Georgia	S	1952
Delta Omega	Bishop College	Dallas, Texas	SW	1955
Delta Omicron	St. Paul's College	Lawrenceville, Virginia	SA	1952
Delta Phi	Ball State College	Muncie, Indiana	MW	1953
Delta Pi	Jackson State College	Jackson, Mississippi	S	1952

Delta Psi		Detroit, Michigan	MW	1954
Delta Rho	Albany State College	Albany, Georgia	S	1952
Delta Tau	Cheyney State Teachers	Cheyney, Pennsylvania	E	1953
Delta Upsilon	Western Michigan University	Kalamazoo, Michigan	MW	1953
Delta Xi	Fayetteville State Teachers	Fayetteville, N. C.	SA	1952
Delta Zeta		Jersey City, N. J.	E	1949
Epsilon	Ohio State University	Columbus, Ohio	MW	1919
Epsilon Alpha	Delaware State College	Dover, Delaware	E	1958
Epsilon Beta	University of Texas	Austin, Texas	SW	1960
Epsilon Delta	Temple University	Philadelphia, Pa.	E	1960
Epsilon Epsilon	Michigan State University	East Lansing, Michigan	MW	1960
Epsilon Eta	Stillman College	Tuscaloosa, Alabama	S	1962
Epsilon Gamma	Pennsylvania State Univ.	University Park, Pa.	E	1960
Epsilon Iota	Ohio University	Athens, Ohio	MW	1963
Epsilon Kappa	Memphis State University	Memphis, Tennessee	S	1963
Epsilon Mu	Kent State University	Kent, Ohio	MW	1964
Epsilon Zeta	Los Angeles State College	Los Angeles, California	FW	1962
Eta	Fort Valley State College	Fort Valley, Georgia	S	1944
Gamma	University of Pennsylvania	Philadelphia, Pa.	E	1918
Gamma Chi	Claflin College	Orangeburg, S. C.	SA	1948
Gamma Epsilon	Texas College	Tyler, Texas	SW	1945
Gamma Gamma	Philander Smith College	Little Rock, Arkansas	SW	1950
Gamma Iota	Hampton Institute	Hampton, Virginia	SA	1945
Gamma Lambda	Johnson C. Smith University	Charlotte, N. C.	SA	1943
Gamma Mu	Knoxville College	Knoxville, Tennessee	S	1947
Gamma Nu	Indiana University	Bloomington, Indiana	MW	1947

Gamma Phi	Winston-Salem College	Winston-Salem, N. C.	SA	1948
Gamma Pi	Allen University	Columbia, South Carolina	SA	1948
Gamma Psi	Tougaloo Southern Christian College	Tougaloo, Mississippi	S	1948
Gamma Rho	St. Augustine's College	Raleigh, North Carolina	SA	1947
Gamma Tau	Tuskegee Institute	Tuskegee, Alabama	S	1947
Gamma Theta		Dayton, Ohio	MW	1946
Gamma Upsilon	Benedict College	Columbia, South Carolina	SA	1948
Gamma Zeta	Morris Brown College	Atlanta, Georgia	S	1942
Iota		Boston, Massachusetts	E	1922
Kappa	University of California	Berkeley, California	FW	1921
Lambda		Chicago, Illinois	MW	1947
Mu	University of Pittsburgh	Pittsburgh, Pennsylvania	E	1921
Nu	University of Michigan	Ann Arbor, Michigan	MW	1921
Pi	University of California	Los Angeles, California	FW	1924
Sigma	Clark College	Atlanta, Georgia	S	1924
Tau	Wayne State University	Detroit, Michigan	MW	1924
Theta	Duquesne University	Pittsburgh, Pennsylvania	E	1946
Upsilon	Univ. of Southern California	Los Angeles, California	FW	1924
Xi	Louisville Municipal College	Louisville, Kentucky	MW	1921
Zeta	University of Cincinnati	Cincinnati, Ohio	MW	1920

MIXED CHAPTERS

Chapter	*Location*	*Region*	*Established*
Alpha Alpha	Kansas City, Missouri	C	1925
Alpha Epsilon	Pittsburgh, Pennsylvania	E	1927
Alpha Omicron	Seattle, Washington	FW	1932
Alpha Phi	Wichita, Kansas	C	1940
Beta Lambda	Toledo, Ohio	MW	1937
Beta Mu	Spring Valley, California	FW	1943
Beta Nu	Gary, Indiana	MW	1938
Beta Omega	Fort Bliss, Texas	SW	1944
Beta Omicron	Corpus Christi, Texas	SW	1947
Beta Phi	Denver, Colorado	C	1938
Beta Psi	Portland, Oregon	FW	1945
Beta Rho	Fort Worth, Texas	SW	1938
Beta Tau	Milwaukee, Wisconsin	MW	1945
Beta Theta	Phoenix, Arizona	FW	1936
Beta Zeta	Pittsburg, Kansas	C	1935
Chi	Indianapolis, Indiana	MW	1925
Delta Lambda	Youngstown, Ohio	MW	1951
Delta Theta	Sacramento, California	FW	1950
Gamma Beta	Topeka, Kansas	C	1944

Gamma Delta	Galveston, Texas	SW	1941
Gamma Kappa	Buffalo, New York	E	1942
Gamma Omicron	Evanston, Illinois	MW	1947
Gamma Xi	Omaha, Nebraska	C	1947
Omega	Cleveland, Ohio	MW	1924
Phi	Des Moines, Iowa	C	1925
Psi	Lawrence, Kansas	C	1925

Index

Adams, Osceola McCarthy, 15, 180
Alaska, 9, 150
Alexander, Catherine Thompson, 22, 24
Alexander, Raymond Pace, 24
Alexander, Sadie Tanner Moselle, 21, 23, 24, 26, 27, 85, 101
Alexander, Virginia M., 21, 24
Alexander, Winona Cargile, 180
Albany Movement, 92
Alpha Chapter, 13, 23
Alpha Kappa Alpha, 11, 13, 16, 96, 99
Alpha Phi Alpha, 96
American Council on Human Rights, 75, 92-93, 98
American Hearing Society, 112
American Library Association, 50
American National Red Cross, 104-105, 109, 121; *see also* Delta Volunteers for Community Service
Anniversary: Fiftieth, 179; Fortieth, 72, 73; *see also* Golden Anniversary
Annual Health Fair, 111
Associate Director, 78
Association for the Study of Negro Life and History, 43
Austin, Elsie, 56, 74
Award: American Library Letter, 51; Julia Bumry Jones, 38; Juliette Derricotte, 38; Thomas Jefferson, 27

Back, Gunner, 73
Banks, Helen Lucas, 21
Barksdale, Marie, 75
Bates, Daisy, 88, 89
Beshears, Helen Dameron, 21
Beta Chapter, 20
Beta Hymn, 21
Bethune, Mary McLeod, 26, 27, 77, 102
Billings, Freddie, 20

Black, Ethel Cuff, 180
Blackburn, Harriett, 160
Book-basket, 46, 52; *see also* Library
Bookmobile, 49, 50, 52; *see also* Library
Bowles, Mrs. Chester, 180
Boyd, Nakomis, 20
Bradley, Dorothy W., 135
Bright, Nellie, 21
Burrell, Fairy Shores, 23
Burroughs, Nannie H., 14, 15
Bush, Joanna M., 88
Butler, Esther, 21
Byrd, David R., 72

Calimese, Ethel, 40
Campbell, Bertha Pitts, 180
CARE (Cooperative for American Remittance to Everywhere), 105, 126, 128
Carrollton (Georgia), 49
Cephas, Marietta, 109
Chania Medical Center, 127
Chapters, 3, 28; undergraduate, 28; graduate, 28; mixed, 28
Chapter: audits, 162-169; dean of pledges, 70; executive committee, 70; local, 69; mailings, 163; meetings, 169; president, 69; program audit, 162, 169; vice president, 70
Cherot, Naomi, 38
Childs, Leroy, 22, 51
Christensen, Ethlyn, 109
Christmas Party, 88-92
Clark, Iolyn Springfield, 20
Cleveland, Grover, 73
Clifford, Paul I., 120
Cobb, Marie Ody, 20
Cobb, Thelma M., 110
College Tuition Fund, 26
Committee Chairmen, 65
Committees, 65-67
  Executive, 70
  Golden Anniversary, 172
  Jewelry, 66
  Library Evaluation, 52
  National Projects, 105, 107, 108, 121, 168, 174
  National Vigilance, 28, 40-41
  Nominating, 64
  Public Affairs, 40, 43, 66
  Publications and Public Relations, 44, 66, 77, 78
  Public Welfare, 66
  Scholarship and Standards, 64, 66, 156; *see also* Standing Committees; *see also* Special Committees
Communications Project, 110
Conference for Counselors, 118
Conover, Marian Hope, 82
Convention, 25, 32, 86; biennial, 25; first national, 23; Golden Jubilee, 181-182; *see also* National Convention
Copeland, Bernice N., 22, 24
Constitution and By-laws, 63
"Counseling Minority Youth," 174

Daniel, Theodora, 44
Davis, Allison, 109, 119, 133, 134
Davis, Hilda, 161
Davis, Myra; *see* Hemmings, Myra Davis
Day, Mrs. J. Edward, 180
Dean of Pledges, 70
Delhi School of Social Work, 126
Delta
  Five Point Projects, 104
  Five Point Program, 59
  Houses, 7
  Journal, 177-178
  Mispah, 88; *see* Songs
  Oath, 14, 84
  Prayer, 88
Delta Chapter, 21
Delta Sigma Theta Public Library, 48
Delta Volunteers for Community Service, 104, 108, 110, 112, 121-124, 168
Densbach, Marian, 109
DePriest, Gladys, 109, 135
Derricotte, Juliette; *see* Award
Dingle, Ann McCary, 24
Dobson, Mildred Griffin, 24
Douglass, Frederick, 73
Douglass, William O., 181
Downs, Mae W., 99
Duncan, Anne E., 45, 47

Eastern Region Pilot Project, 122

Eisenhower, Dwight D., 73
Edwards, Cecil, 111
Emancipation Proclamation, 4
Epsilon Chapter, 22
Executive Board, 63-65
Executive Committee, 70
Executive Director, 64, 66, 74, 75-76

Faubus, Orville, 89
Fellowship, 81
Ferguson, Helen, 20
Fields, Violetta London, 21
Fiftieth Anniversary Birthday Celebration, 179
First National President, 24
Five Point Program, 170-172
Five Point Project, 107, 108, 109, 112, 137, 174
Founders, 15-17, 72, 84, 179, 182
Founders Day, 12, 84, 162
Founding, 11-13
Ford Vanette Bookmobile, 50
Fortune, Hilda O., 160
Foster, Edith, 51
Foster, Vera, 109, 132
Fortieth Anniversary, 72, 73
Franklin County (North Carolina), 47, 48
Fraternal Organizations, 92, 96
Frazier, E. Franklin, 143, 144, 149, 153
Freedom Rider, 91
"Freedom Rides," 155
"Freedom Village," 126
Fund for Freedom, 101

Gamma Chapter, 21
Ghana, 126
Girl Scouts of America, 105, 109, 121; *see also* Delta Volunteers for Community Service
Glass, Margaret, 20
Golden Agers Parties, 34
Golden Anniversary, 153, 169-171, 180-181, 182; committee, 169, 172, 173; fund, 172, 173; gleaner, 173; goals, 170; luncheon, 179; pioneers, 173; years, 162
Grand Chapter, 13, 23, 24, 28, 30, 62-63
Grand Historian, 66
Grand Journalist, 66
Granger, Lester, 102
Greek Symbol, 13
Gregory, Montgomery, 16
Green, Edith, 179, 180
Green, Elizabeth Gross, 21
Gunner, Frances, 20

Habein, Margaret, 161
Haiti, 9
Hall, Lester, 135
Hanley, Alberta, 23
Harlee, Alma M., 87
Harris, Patricia Roberts, 74, 75, 99, 105, 132, 140
Harrison-Black-Fletcher Bill, 42
Headquarters Staff, 74-76
Hearing Conservation Project, 112
Height, Dorothy I., 38, 50, 51, 53, 74, 103, 126, 148, 149, 169
Helphant, Kenneth, 109, 132, 134
Hemmings, Myra Davis, 13, 180
Henry, E. P., 135
Higginbotham, Gwendolyn H., 71, 169
High, Stanley, 73
Hodges, Mrs. Luther, 180
Hollis Burke Frissell Library, 113
Honorary Members, 14, 15, 102
Hoover, Theressa, 160
Horne, Lena, 90
Howard University, 5, 11, 13

"I-Check," 177
Immediate Past President, 65
Incorporate, 12
Incorporation, 13, 61-62, 98
International, 87
International Project, 105, 108, 124-130, 168, 174
"Invest in Education," 85; *see also* May Week

Jabberwock, 82-84, 162, 166-167
Jackson, Geraldine, 24
Jackson, Kara, 109, 132, 174, 175
Jackson, Nelson, 109
James, Lucia, 109
January thirteen, 12, 84
Jersild, Arthur T., 109, 132, 133
Jewelry Committee, 66

Job Analysis Commission, 53-54
Job Analysis and Opportunities, 36, 43, 53, 55
Job Opportunities, 53-59, 105, 108, 110, 112, 117, 149, 168, 174; Conferences, 117, 119; Project, 58, 101, 108
Joint Committee on National Recovery, 35
Johnson, Ada Hyde, 21
Johnson, Anna R.; *see* Julian, Anna Johnson
Johnson, Charles, 73
Johnson, Letitia, 75, 132
Johnson, Lyndon B., 181
Johnson, Robert, 160
Jones, Eloise, 75
Jones, J. B., 178
Jones, Julia Bumry, 38; *see also* Award
Jones, Virginia Lacey, 46, 47, 50
Journal, 77-78, 110; *see also* Publications
Judiciary & Standards Boards, 66
Julian, Anna Johnson, 13, 61, 97

Kappa Alpha Psi, 96
Kennedy, John F., 179
Kenya (Africa), 90, 127
King, Marion, 91
King, Marjorie, 109
King, Martin Luther, 154
King Street Library, 52

LaFolliette, Mrs., 16
Lameck, Lucy, 127, 128
Lampkin, Daisy E., 71, 72
Leadership Institutes, 137
Lee, Mollie Houston, 46, 47
Legal Adviser, 65
Lewis, Charlotte, 44, 99, 109
Liberia (Africa), 9, 150
Library Evaluation Committee, 52
Library Project, 55; *see* Library Service
Library Service, 36, 45-53, 105, 108, 110-116, 168
Lincoln, Abraham, 182
Little Rock, 89; *see also* Christmas Party
Live Wires, 88; *see also* Songs
Loucheim, Katie, 180
L'Ouverture, Toussaint, 101
Lucas, Corinne, 135

Marsh, Alma, 132
Martin, Ruby, 19, 20
Mason, Beatrice, 20
Maynard, Hazel Shaw, 24
May Week, 25-26, 72, 85, 162
McCleave, Florence Talbert, 27, 88
McCullers, Mildred, 48
MEDICO (Medical International Cooperation Organization), 105
MEDICARE, 105
Members-at-Large, 165, 171
Menninger, Karl, 131
Mental Health Project, 105, 108, 112, 130-136, 168
Mental Health Workshop, 131
Middleton, Jimmie Bugg, 16, 180
Montagu, Ashley, 152
Montgomery Bus Boycott, 154
Morehead, Ola Calhoun, 21
Moselle, Sadie Tanner; *see* Alexander, Sadie Tanner Moselle
Mungai Maternity Wing (Kenya), 105
Mungai, Njorge, 90
Myers, Leila N., 135

National Association for Mental Health, 105, 109
National Mental Health Association, 109
Nabrit, Mrs. James, 180
NAACP (National Association for the Advancement of Colored People), 43, 88, 100, 101, 154; Leadership Conferences, 101
National Association of Colored Women, 14
National Association of Women's Clubs, 27
National Board, 8, 151
National Business League, 27
National Committee Against Discrimination in Housing, 105
National Community Chests and Councils, 121; *see also* Delta Volunteers for Community Service

National Convention, 24, 30, 31, 63, 68, 85, 110, 153; Chairman, 64; Director, 76
National Council of Negro Women, 27, 90, 102
National Headquarters, 64, 65, 71-73; campaign, 71
National Hymn, 27, 88; *see* Songs
National Interfraternal Council, 96, 97
National Library Project, 116; *see* Library Service
National Office, 146
National Officers, 137, 146-147
National Pan Hellenic Council, 97, 98, 100, 146
National Projects Committee, 105, 107, 108, 121, 168, 174
National President, 64
National Projects, 36
National Recovery, 40
National Scholarship Award Fund, 37
National Scholarship Loan Fund, 37
National Scholarship Service and Fund for Negro Students, 39
National Students Association of International Relations Clubs, 105
National Urban League, 43, 100, 101, 105, 109, 117, 118, 121, 154; *see also* Delta Volunteers for Community Service
National Vigilance Committee, 28, 40
Negro Colleges, 29
Negro College Women, 3
Negro Heroes, 101
Negro Sorority, 158
Nelson, Alice Dunbar, 21, 27, 88
Nelson, Eunice, 75
New Deal, 35
New Deal for Delta, 35
New Delhi School of Social Work, 38
Newhouse, Annie Singleton, 20
Newsletter, 77, 78, 177; *see also* Publications
Nineteen hundred and thirteen, 5
Ninth Grade Clinics, 118-119
Noble, Jeanne L., 109, 132, 145, 156, 170, 178
Nominating Committee, 64
Officers Round Table, 170; *see also* Round Table
Official Directory, 77; *see also* Publications
Official Pledge Pin, 23
Omega Omega, 27
Omega Psi Phi, 96

Pan-Hellenic, Inc., 146
Parents' Winged Horse, 116; *see* Library Service
Parents' Clinics, 118
Parent Teacher Associations, 34, 35
Past National President, 103
Peal, Mrs. S. Edward, 180
Pegasus, 113
Pelham, G. Dorothy, 27
Pelham, Gabrielle, 14
Penn, Eloise, 88
Penn, Madree; *see* White, Madree Penn
Personnel Committee, 64
Peterson, Esther, 180
Phi Beta Sigma, 96
Pilot Center, 111
Placement Chairman, 124
Pledges, 70
Plummer, Bernadette, 109
Polk, Julia, 21
President's Committee on Civil Rights, 24
Price, Margaret, 178
Prince Edward County, 90
Program Planning Committee, 69
Public Affairs Committee, 40, 43; Subcommittee, 44, 45
Publications, 76-78; Constitution & By-laws, 76; Grand Officers Handbook, 76; Official Handbook, 76; Pyramid Handbook, 76; Ritual, 76; Songbook, 76
Publications and Public Relations Committee, 44, 77, 78; Public Affairs Subcommittee, 99
Public Relations Counsel, 173
Public Service, 6, 171
Public Service Organization, 5
Public Service Projects, 83
Purpose, 62
Pushkin, Alexander, 101
Pyramids, 70

Quander, Nellie, 12

Radden, Thelma, 109
Ray, Wilma H., 168, 177
Reclamation, 171
Reeves, Elizabeth, 44
Regional Conference, 27, 68
Regional Directors, 28, 65, 67, 68-69, 137
Regions, 67-69
Republic of Haiti, 125-126, 150
Richard B. Harrison Library, 46
Richards, Helen, 87
Ride the Winged Horse, 113-114, 115; *see also* Library Service
Riley, Elnora, 135
Rioch, Janet, 109, 132, 133, 134
Robertson, Mamie Diggs, 21
Robinson, Harriette, 24
Roosevelt, Franklin D., 35
Round Table, 172, 174; *see also* Officers Round Table
Rucker, Mary, 109

Sander, Bernice, 20
Sanford, Nevitt, 161
Sanjuan, Mrs. Pedro A., 180
Scholarship
  Aid, 36-39
  Board, 37
  Fund, 167
  Program, 26
Scholarship & Standards Committee, 64, 66, 156; Chairman, 171
Scholarship Award Fund, 26
Scholarships, 83, 167
Scholastic Grades, 26, 36
Search for Future Scientists, 118
Second Vice-president, 64
Secretary, 64
Senbach, Marian, 132
Shaw, Esther Popel, 35, 40
Shippen, Eliza P., 16, 180
Smith, Virginia B., 109
Social Action, 39-45
Social Action & Education, 44
Songs, 87-88
Southard, Helen F., 177
Southern Regional Project, 111-112
Special Committees: Auditing, 65; Convention, 65; Credentials, 65; Nominating, 65; *see also* Committees
Standards, 26, 36
Standing Committees: Finance, 65; National Projects, 65; Personnel, 65; Publications & Public Relations, 65; Scholarship & Standards, 65; *see also* Committees
Stevenson, George, 109, 132, 133, 134
Student Emergency Fund, 93
Suffragettes, 16
"Sunday Winged Arts," 116; *see* Library Service
Sweetheart Song, 88; *see* Songs
Sweetheart Waltz, 88; *see* Songs

Talbert, Florence C.; *see* McCleave, Florence Talbert
Tanganyika (Africa), 127
Tanganyika African National Union, 127
Tanner, Henry O., 24
Terrell, Mary Church, 7, 14, 73
The Delta, 26; *see* Publications
Toms, Florence Letcher, 17, 180
Tours, 86-87
Traditional Delta Program, 162
Travis, Brenda, 91
Treasurer, 65
Truman, Harry S., 24
Tuskegee Project, 114

Undergraduate Coordinator, 64
UNESCO (United Nations Educational, Scientific, and Cultural Organization), 105, 128
United Community Funds and Councils, 105, 109
United States Assembly of Youth, 105
Urban League: *see* National Urban League

Vassar Conference, 66
Vice President, 70
Vick, Hollis, 109
Vigilance and Public Affairs, 36, 39, 55; Committee, 41; *see also* Social Action

Vines, Harriette Alexander, 21
Voting Delegates, 63

Washington, Booker T., 101
Washington, Vivian, 147
Watkins, Maude L., 46, 109
Weaver, Wertie Blackwell, 180
Wheatley, Phyllis, 101
Wherry, Franklin, 135
White, Alberta, 88
White House Conference, 105
White, Madree Penn, 13, 19, 20, 180
White, Phila Ann McGillery, 22
Williams, Clara B., 178
Williams, Mrs. G. Mennon, 180
Wirtz, Mrs. W. Willard, 180
Wise, Max, 120, 161
World University Service, 105
Woods, Geraldine P., 171
Workshop on Minority Youth, 176; *see* Job Opportunities
Wright, Bertrell C., 99
Wright, Sara-Alyce, 137, 157

Yancey Commission on Undergraduate Development, 7, 142, 157-162, 169
Yancey, Sadie M., 156, 157
YMCA (Young Men's Christian Association), 129
Young Adult Council of Social Welfare Assembly, 105
Young, Edith Motte, 15, 21
YWCA (Young Women's Christian Association), 38, 53, 56, 104, 109, 121, 137, 177; *see also* Delta Volunteers for Community Service

Zeta Phi Beta, 97